FIGHTING
MALEVOLENT
SPIRITS

© Samantha E. Harris

About the Author

Samantha Harris was born in Ann Arbor, Michigan, and now lives with her two English Bulldogs (Jack and Annabelle) and pet snake (Sir Hiss) in rural Michigan. Samantha started her own mini farm with nine hens, one rooster (Rufio), and four dwarf dairy goats that now contribute to a milk-share farm.

She established her award-winning videography company during her senior year at Michigan State University and enjoys spending her free time creating art and jewelry. Samantha loves growing organic food and supports sustainable and green alternatives. As an advocate for Native American civil rights, she produced a short documentary to bring awareness to contemporary indigenous and environmental issues.

Samantha enjoys teaching others how to help and protect themselves spiritually and feels that everyone should be entitled to such knowledge no matter their religious beliefs. She continues her work in the metaphysical field with house blessings, writing, public speaking, and television appearances about the paranormal. Samantha's retirement dream is to open a charming metaphysical store one day.

FIGHTING
MALEVOLENT
SPIRITS

SAMANTHA E. HARRIS

A DEMONOLOGIST'S DARKEST ENCOUNTERS

Llewellyn Publications
Woodbury, Minnesota

FIRST EDITION
First Printing, 2014

Cover art: iStockphoto.com/8183058/dorioconnell
iStockphoto.com/2972092/13Claudio13
iStockphoto.com/14090553/Bliznetsov
iStockphoto.com/14554223/DonNichols
iStockphoto.com/8187671/zeremski
iStockphoto.com/15660141/Benimage
Cover design by Kevin R. Brown
Llewellyn Publications is a registered trademark of Llewellyn Worldwide, Ltd.

Library of Congress Cataloging-in-Publication Data
Harris, Samantha E., 1988–
  Fighting malevolent spirits : a demonologist's darkest encounters /
Samantha E. Harris. — First edition.
      pages   cm
  ISBN 978-0-7387-3697-6
1. Demonology. 2. Occultism. 3. Parapsychology. I. Title.
BF1531.H37 2013
133.4'2—dc23
                                          2013042068

Llewellyn Worldwide Ltd. does not participate in, endorse, or have any authority or responsibility concerning private business transactions between our authors and the public.

All mail addressed to the author is forwarded, but the publisher cannot, unless specifically instructed by the author, give out an address or phone number.

Any Internet references contained in this work are current at publication time, but the publisher cannot guarantee that a specific location will continue to be maintained. Please refer to the publisher's website for links to authors' websites and other sources.

Llewellyn Publications
A Division of Llewellyn Worldwide Ltd.
2143 Wooddale Drive
Woodbury, MN 55125-2989, U.S.A.
www.llewellyn.com

Printed in the United States of America

This book is dedicated to our Creator,
my family, friends, and loved ones.
I would also like to thank the skeptics and critics
for the motivation you have instilled in me. I love you all.

Contents

PREFACE

I became interested in the paranormal at a young age—a result of numerous enigmatic experiences. Preceding my discovery of dark entities, I grew up in rural Michigan with a loving, normal family (or as normal as families can get!).

The only thing unusual about my family is that every generation on my mother's side of the family seems to possess a psychic gift of some sort (some view it as a burden). A few years ago we discovered home videos from when I was about three years old, making predictions about what was inside a wrapped Christmas present. I excitedly claimed "I'm psychic!" after opening the predicted item. I later began having "death premonitions" in the form of dreams, and within hours or days the prediction would sadly come true.

On one particular occasion I dreamt I was in my bedroom, standing at the foot of the bed when the phone rang. The green caller ID light glowed and my grandmother's name flashed across the screen. I picked up the phone and my grandma was sobbing on the other end of the line. "Cody is dying." Cody was her much-loved Golden Retriever who had also belonged to her late husband. I awoke from the dream, completely forgetting about the vision until later in the afternoon. A sense of déjà vu came over me as I stood at the foot of the bed. The phone rang. I instantly remembered the dream I had earlier that morning and cringed as the exact scene unfolded before me in real time. Grandma was hysterically crying, "Cody has cancer." Everything was identical to my dream but the wording had slightly changed.

Months later I was in my morning art class in high school when I suddenly became overwhelmed with sadness and grief. I excused myself into the art supply closet and inexplicably cried. I felt confused and wondered if I was bipolar or why I had been overcome with such extreme emotions.

I called my mother to ask if everything was okay; by this age I was just starting to learn that when these "emotions" occurred, something was likely happening to someone dear to me. My mother informed me that only two or three minutes before they had euthanized Cody.

I believe I had felt my grandma's emotions and pain through some sort of unseen connection or telepathy. I had no previous knowledge that Cody was to be put down that day and at what time.

Then, weird events happened just before my beloved grandpa died from an overdose of chemotherapy at the University of Michigan. Even my sibling was witness to the strange occurrences of shadows sinking through the floor and disembodied voices.

In no way do I consider myself a "psychic" or a "medium"—I believe that everyone is born with a sixth sense; however, in Western and industrialized cultures, we learn to tune out this gift. I have psychic experiences, as demonstrated in this book, but have not harnessed my personal abilities to the level that many psychics and mediums have.

Like many children, I had felt the presence of darker things in my bedroom at night but never had a name for them and didn't understand. Once in a blue moon I would see spirits in the form of shadows and hear incorporeal voices; some of them were nice, others were not.

When I was about nine years old I was taking a shower and heard a serpentlike voice hiss out my name in the bathroom, "*Ssssamanttttha.*" I closed my eyes and waited for it to leave. It felt dark but soon departed; this gave me a brief glimpse of what I would battle in the future.

In seventh grade I attended a summer camp in northern Michigan. While I was there I had been busy taking pictures on a cheap Kodak disposable camera. At night around the campfire the usual ghost stories were told and claims that the camp was haunted were overlooked in my mind. Every camp seems to claim that it is haunted, and I took it all in with a grain of salt. In fact, I didn't pay much attention to it and forgot about the ghostly side of the grounds.

One late afternoon my friends Melissa and Angela and I were walking around the camp with some other girls and decided to visit the old theater building. Inside was a stage, some back rooms, and an old couch in front of a corkboard. I took a couple of pictures of the girls goofing off when I began to feel an odd sensation. The air became dense. I felt like I was being watched. None of the other girls seemed to notice, so I ignored it the best I could. As the girls sat on the lone couch, Angela kicked her legs out in a comical way and I snapped a photograph.

Weeks passed. One day, as I sat in my room at home, I felt overwhelmingly compelled to look through the pictures of my time at camp. I had previously glanced at the pictures briefly, but this time I found myself looking for something—I didn't even know what! I turned the page of the album and saw what my intuition was guiding me towards: A full apparition of a woman stood behind the girls on the couch in the photograph. The spirit seemed to be resting her head upon her hand and smirking as if enjoying Angela's ridiculous pose in the picture.

I ran into the kitchen to show my mother and she was taken aback.

We wanted explanations and soon headed to the local camera store in town. One of the men, a professional photographer and lab technician who had worked there for over thirty years, examined the photograph. He said it was not a double exposure, nor a reflection of any light or of me. The corkboard was not laminated or surrounded by Plexiglas at that time and the image of the woman looked nothing like me—I was the only person there could be a reflection of! The ghostly woman even appeared in the photograph's negative.

My mother and I didn't know what to think, but we were extremely excited about the discovery.

The camp picture is available on the Michigan Paranormal Research Association's website, www.MichiganPRA.com. The website also has other possible evidence I have gathered from cases and investigations, as mentioned in this book.

After the camp episode, I was hungry for more answers, knowledge, truth, and experiences. I began researching case studies and reading many books—more than my bookshelves could hold!

My research and training has always been a solo experience for me. I am constantly learning and my education is never complete. In my college years I began looking for mentors to help guide me. I found few advisors and finally accepted that spiritual warfare was a path I would walk alone on this earth, but with spiritual guidance directing me.

Each experience has taught me something new and I always welcome fresh opportunities to discuss or demonstrate the paranormal with the public. Teaching and lecturing is something I also thoroughly enjoy and I have presented at various conferences, universities, and venues in Michigan after fourteen years, and counting, of research.

After racking up cases under my belt and going public with Michigan Paranormal Research Association's (M.P.R.A.) endeavors, Hollywood began sniffing us out and we were soon faced with reality TV.

In 2009 I was offered a television series contract for the direct sequel to *Paranormal State* for the A&E Network, featured on the Travel Channel's *Most Terrifying Places in America* in 2010, and in 2012 one of our cases debuted on *A Haunting* (a Discovery Channel series that aired on the Destination America network). I have been contacted over the years by William Shatner's *Weird or What*, A&E's *My Ghost Story*, Sy-Fy's *School Spirits* and *Paranormal Witness*, and more.

Reality is not what happens on "reality TV," in fact, many reality series are staged, prompted, and guided at the hands of the producers. I do not mean to imply that *all* reality TV shows are artificial but an unfortunate number are misleading. Ironically, many of my paranormal encounters happened off-camera while filming for television and were more interesting than the intended plot!

One such incident happened while filming our pilot at the Holly Hotel for the direct sequel to *Paranormal State* on A&E (long before *The New Class* run-off was produced). I remember saying out loud, "Commencing blackout time" before we cut out the lights. (We were asked to create a variation of "Dead-Time" for our sequel; *Paranormal State* fans will understand this.)

Shortly after the darkness filled the room, I heard the cameraman, Bob, blurt out a startled phrase. "What the hell?" One of the spirits had apparently walked up to Bob and blatantly kicked his camera while he was trying to film an eerie shot from an angle on the floor. In the recording, we heard the boom microphone being struck. No one was near Bob at the time of the event and the incident could not be mistaken.

My former partner Carl O'Toole and I knew it was going to be an interesting night of filming at the Holly Hotel. Bob had been a disbeliever but now seemed to have an unspoken respect for the Holly Hotel and the paranormal.

Later that evening one of the decorative dishes hanging in the parlor area disappeared on its own accord. The owner of the Holly Hotel questioned the staff—no one had removed the item and it hung nearly eight or ten feet from the ground. Bringing in a ladder would have been noticeable and the parlor bartender stated that no one had been in the room during her shift. Strange things were always happening at the Holly Hotel.

The production company we were working with had produced *Paranormal State*, *Laguna Beach*, and *The Hills*, in addition to a possible upcoming show about "hot girls" investigating the paranormal. I was concerned about their ability to respect the paranormal and hesitant to sign a contract with them. I became more concerned when they discussed the possibility of bringing in another paranormal investigator and having us pretend she was originally from M.P.R.A. I am not one to fabricate things or to play "pretend," but it also did not seem terribly harmful … just artificial. Right before heading to Connecticut to film our first actual episode, the producers slipped us a thirteen-episode contract agreement.

Mick, the producer, tried coaxing me into signing the document with a few days' notice. I wanted more time to review the contract. I wasn't willing to sell my soul for some TV show to gain publicity, to lower my personal and ethical standards, and I certainly was not going to accept the idea of fabricating evidence or reenacting paranormal events for the show as stated in the contract. However, I was willing to co-operate on several things.

Everything came to a halt when I asked the producers how negotiable the contract was, seeing as the first page stated "negotiable contract." I learned that negotiable doesn't really mean negotiable. We had jumped through so many hoops that I started to feel like Echo the Dolphin from the Sega Genesis video game.

I remember sitting at the International Center on campus with Carl during a lunch break. We were watching CNN news on one of the TV monitors in the lounge area. I had been begging God to give me a "sign" about whether I should continue with this TV series idea or call it quits. I didn't want to be a sellout, and I took our work very seriously. We wanted to help people and perhaps viewers could learn to help themselves and others through watching our show.

I glanced up at the TV after taking another bite of my Chinese food when I read "Call Mick" on the ticker tagline of the monitor. It kept passing over the screen: "Call Mick." I thought it was odd and pointed it out to Carl. We both laughed. "That's really weird … Well, maybe you should," Carl suggested.

Later that day, I feverishly searched CNN's website for a show or news blip titled "Call Mick" and never found anything. Sometimes God works in mysterious ways, so I called Mick.

Something that bothered me about the controversial contract was that it was "effective throughout this universe." I couldn't help but laugh. *What if I wanted to participate in a dif-*

ferent show in a separate galaxy... would that still violate the terms? Finally, I decided it was more important to protect my group members than become confined to a TV show.

I was somewhat heartbroken that the show wouldn't pan out; I wanted to share our solutions to hauntings with the world so people could help themselves, but at the same time I was learning about the troubles with Hollywood.

Fast-forward a year or two and we were dealing with another set of producers. My chemistry with Carl worked great through the medium of TV, and we were happy to be filming again. We found ourselves back at the Holly Hotel working with this new production company for the Travel Channel's *Most Terrifying Places in America*. It was also an interesting experience.

Again, we jumped through more hoops. I began scouting for actors for the show's reenactment segment weeks prior to the filming and volunteered to do the makeup for one of the actors. I always went out of my way to help with filming. Being a videographer and producer myself, I understood the process and hard work involved in productions. But alas, Hollywood is Hollywood, and like an infectious disease it will corrupt anything that is "trendy," such as the paranormal, even if it requires compromising ethics and respect.

For example, prior to filming, one of my honorary group members, Lisa, was suffering from severe fibromyalgia and had just recently undergone a mastectomy. After begging her doctor, she received permission to come with us to film at the Holly Hotel for the episode. I remember she was heavily medicated and was dozing in and out of consciousness—she amazed me and was such a strong woman.

I was absolutely distraught watching the final airing of the episode, realizing that she and all the other group members had been completely cut out of the episode! Instead, one of the producers pretended to be a visitor at the hotel and during his segment of the episode he included a false story about an experience at the Holly Hotel. Again, Hollywood is a strange and indifferent world.

Reality TV shows also take words out of context. They attempted to make the Holly Hotel seem as if it were the horrifying Stanley Hotel in *The Shining*. The Holly Hotel is actually a friendly and charming restaurant.

Since then I have been contacted by numerous production companies, producers, television and radio shows, and various news outlets. I always enjoy working with the media not because of fame or fortune (and it should be noted that there is no fortune to be made in reality shows or docu-dramas), but because I try to expand the minds of the producers to demonstrate that the media has only scraped the surface of "paranormal television." There is so much more to film, document, and share with the public. Personally, I'd like to see the media focus on the positive and healing side of the paranormal more, much like *Long Island Medium* and other shows, which are loving and reassuring of life after death. There is so much negative junk on television; it would be nice to see the fun and positive side once in a while!

———

Working with the paranormal community is a continuous lesson as well. On a rare occasion I will network with other individuals in the field to participate in a case or to compare notes. There are both benefits and setbacks to working with others in the paranormal field. You can meet some amazing and experienced individuals, but you can also run into politics, ego, and religious battles, or territorial issues. Human error will wiggle its way into any field of study, and as shown in the following cases in this book, I've had both wonderful and alarming experiences working with others. My quest for the truth is never finished and each person I encounter helps me grow closer to knowing.

INTRODUCTION

As a paranormal investigator and demonologist, I never grew up thinking about battling demons nor did I really give the concept of "demons" a thought; however, the lifestyle of fighting these entities chose me. I was soon guided down the path to helping others and found myself offering solutions to hauntings and demonic oppression outside of conventional religious methods. Frustrated by the lack of help from churches, many individuals began seeking my help as a last resort.

Handling demonic cases has altered the way I view myself, the world, and the safety of those around me, and yet it has also enlightened me through the reward of helping others. God and I have an agreement, or so I like to think—I will always work for Him and battle his enemies as long as my loved ones and animals are never harmed as a consequence of my actions. To this day we both have kept our word and I intend to honor our Creator for as long as my soul exists.

Oddly enough, I do not adhere to one religion and instead am a very spiritual individual. I was raised as a Christian but have come to respect all religions and beliefs. I believe in a Christ-figure because of an out-of-body experience I had after a surgery and the effectiveness "Christ" has on the demonic, but I do not follow mainstream religion.

If you were to combine an exorcist, demonologist, paranormal investigator, counselor, and a spiritual healer, you would discover something along the lines of how I function. I became a reverend through a universal ministry and incorporate various methods in the removal of both human spirit and demonic hauntings. Demons exist in all civilizations around the world and I have found, through years of studying various cultures and religions, that there is more than one way to remove them, which proves to me that God transcends any specific denomination or religion.

I have researched the paranormal for over fourteen years, since I was about eleven years old, and have come to practice the art of spiritual healing for many distraught families. As of early 2013, I have performed over eighty cleansings for families and individuals experiencing a severely negative haunting.

Surprisingly, I was a pretty normal child—aside from my fascination with spiritualism and the metaphysical. In high school, as the newspaper's entertainment editor, I wrote articles about local paranormal hauntings and crazy adventures at rock concerts. I unintentionally created an odd reputation for myself, but no one seemed to mind. One thing that has always remained true about me is my desire to fight for and protect those who can't defend themselves, both humans and animals alike. This aspect of my soul is what led me into some of the darkest places of this world in an effort to help others. I never really knew what I wanted to do with my life, but I did know that I wanted to assist others and to make a positive impact on the world.

During my college career I began performing house cleansings for individuals and families—it gave me the sense of helping and healing others I so deeply craved.

In college I studied abnormal psychology and received my B.A. from Michigan State University (go Green!) in communications and media studies in May of 2011. I am delighted that our society has progressed beyond demonizing mental illnesses and claiming individuals were simply possessed; however, I have witnessed instances in which modern science cannot simply explain away certain phenomena.

For the skeptics reading this, thank you for taking the time to read this book. I respect skeptics because unless you have truly experienced something, you can't really believe in it. However, if a person does not go out of their way to experience or research something, such as demonology, they are likely not going to encounter it. And thank goodness for that! If you are a true skeptic, then this book may persuade you to believe in the supernatural. If you are a disbeliever and already have your mind made up … well, this might just be an amusing book for you to read. Either way, enjoy! This is not a book to provide scientific proof that demons exist but rather to share true accounts of demonic hauntings and the evidence that I have gathered.

It is said that nearly three out of four Americans believe in the paranormal realm, and yet some fear being ostracized for even discussing such matters. More often than not, the stranger next to you in the grocery store or movie theater has experienced something "unexplainable."

It is important to note that I do not demonize the paranormal; not everything is evil and ghosts are not demons. I have seen very powerful and loving divine beings that have healed and consoled others, but I do know and acknowledge the darkness that exists in this world on the opposite side of the paranormal spectrum.

Reading this book and fighting demons does not require a certain faith. I believe we are all children of God and can act as spiritual warriors on His behalf. Individuals should respect the concept of evil and the demonic, and never antagonize or welcome in such spirits.

From this book, you will learn different methods of self-protection, how to remove hauntings, and you will gain an understanding of demonic entities through actual accounts. These stories may disturb you, as there are graphic details I have chosen to include; I feel it is important to remain truthful and realistic. These are true stories about real families, real clients, and demons that I believe to be very real.

To respect the privacy of individuals and families, the names mentioned in this book have been changed; however, the stories remain true. It should also be noted that in this book I may refer to "God" as Great Spirit, Creator, God, Lord, and so on. Readers are welcome to substitute "God" with their preferred name for a Higher Power.

QUESTIONS & ANSWERS

What is a demon?

In theory and according to holy texts, a demon is a fallen angel that betrayed God. Some cultures believe they are evil spirits who have always roamed the earth in spirit form and were never "good" to begin with. Others believe they are "tricksters" or spirits that exist as a result of our bad human behavior. Regardless, almost every single culture and religion around the world recognizes a negative spirit or entity that preys on humans for a number of reasons.

I think that demons are universal spirits, meaning they are experienced globally and cross-culturally and are very ancient beings. I have learned and witnessed that their main objective is to destroy and break down relationships, emotions, finances, health, and most of all, to isolate their targeted victims. They feed off of negative energy and wreak havoc in order to thrive. If they can destroy one's faith in Spirit and God, all the better.

From my research, demons seem to exploit and corrupt any positive or enjoyable human experience (i.e., relationships, sex, happiness, etc.) seemingly out of jealousy and hate. They are intelligent creatures that should not be underestimated.

Never antagonize a demon or challenge it. Simply ignore the entity and command it out in the name of God until you are able to have a cleansing performed. It should be noted that demons are not ghosts or human spirits, although they can disguise themselves as such. Most hauntings consist of human spirits, but on occasion we will find that a demon(s) is residing in the house. A list of characteristics and telltale signs to differentiate between human spirits and demons is given next.

How can you tell if it's a demon?

Demons usually have a set of characteristics and behaviors that make them identifiable for us. More often than not, demons will come into the person or family's life subtly and then get progressively worse. In the beginning, they are frequently mistaken for being a human ghost, until things turn violent, aggressive, and dark. Most human spirits do not have the energy and power to cause physical harm or throw large objects as seen in demonic cases. Demons may exhibit "poltergeist" activity by throwing objects, moving furniture, making messes, screaming, and so on. Here is what most of our demonic cases have consisted of (not all characteristics must match for the spirit to be demonic):

- Hearing: Growling, scratching and banging on the walls, knocking, feathers fluttering, pig grunts and squeals, cat howling, wolf howling, hissing, shrieking, screaming, voices and singing coming from the heating vents, hooves clicking, sinister laughing or chuckling, mimicking of family members' voices, voices instructing the individual to harm themselves or others, and to do inappropriate or harmful things, etc.

- Seeing: Tall and lanky figures, shrouded or cloaked silhouettes, shadows, black clouds or matter that move on the floor, walls, or ceiling, evil faces, writing on the mirrors, floors, or walls that may be threatening, symbols, footprints in the shape of hooves, claws, or inhuman feet.

  Sometimes demons will actually appear as a sinister human spirit. Essentially, they are shape-shifters and can really appear as anything (fake angels, black dogs, children, creatures, beasts, and so on).

- Smelling: Sulfur or rotten eggs, burning, burnt rubber or plastics, decaying or rotting odors. Any foul smell is usually associated with demonic entities. Smells will appear without a logical cause and can become overpowering, sometimes leading to nausea or fainting.

How do demons come into someone's life?

There are numerous reasons why an individual or a family may begin to experience a demonic haunting or demonic oppression. Demons prey on the weak and the ill—anything that weakens you is something a demon capitalizes on. The most common causes I have seen in our cases are alcoholism, substance abuse, sexual abuse, domestic violence, depression and anxiety issues, chronic illness, and unprotected meddling with the occult.

Some religions will teach you that *any* involvement with the metaphysical will create an opportunity for the demonic; however, I disagree. After encountering numerous cases, I have the following views on astrology, psychics, and Ouija boards:

1) To those who believe astrology is a satanic practice, I like to reference the Three Wise Men, who were astrologers. I do not believe it is evil to study God's amazing creation, the universe and stars, in the form of astrology, unless you put it *above* God. I have never encountered a demonic case stemming from the reading of "daily horoscopes." Some people use divination as a way of connecting *with* God, much like when people attend church to feel connected with God. Worship can be demonstrated in numerous ways and it is important to be accepting of other cultures, practices, and religions.

2) I do not believe legitimate psychics or mediums are evil—I have heard some of the most loving and compassionate messages that only brought closure and relief to the client (in no way was it a deception of evil). These messages confirmed life after death and the existence of God and Heaven, strengthening the client's faith. I have the gift of being able to discern spirits, so I actually sense evil when it is present, and during these psychic readings nothing but God and love was present. Being able to give readings is a gift from God and, for

those who may think it's sinister, is listed in Corinthians in the Bible. Undoubtedly, there are some phony mediums and psychics out there who take advantage of others, but if you find a genuine one, you will know that it is God working through them.

3) I personally do not use Ouija boards, but I believe that spirit communication can be accomplished safely; however, many individuals do not take the additional precautionary efforts to ensure their safety. I firmly believe everyone should use an opening and closing prayer when using message boards, because you can unknowingly welcome in an entity that may or may not be demonic. I have had several cases in which Ouija boards were used, but none of the families thought to protect themselves with a prayer like, "No evil or negative entities are allowed to speak or connect with us, only positive and loving spirits may communicate. In God's name we pray. Amen."

I like to compare people using an Ouija board to being a telemarketer—you're calling all these phone numbers and you have no idea what type of person is going to answer the phone. It is a very dangerous situation to be in, especially when adolescents use the board under the influence of substances, making themselves even more vulnerable. Have respect for the dangers and use a protection prayer or stay away from an Ouija board entirely.

There are other routes in which demons can enter someone's life, but they are much less common than the above reasons. Sometimes demons are drawn to a person's aura, energy, and personality. Demons can also be attracted to someone from a public place like a hospital and prey on that individual during their recovery or illness.

Surprisingly, there have been cases involving rape victims. If they didn't receive adequate counseling or closure, the demon was drawn in through their resentment, anger, and depression over the incident.

Death of a family member, friend, or loved one can also create negative feelings of anguish, anger, loss of faith in God, and other problematic emotions that can attract a demon. Fully experiencing and accepting death or a tragic event is therapeutic; however, if the negative feelings continue for a prolonged period of time, an individual may be putting themselves more at risk.

I have also studied cases of "ancestral demonic oppression" in which the demonic entity is inherited through the family line over the years—meaning the demon attaches itself to different family members as time passes.

Satanic worship is also a direct way to attach a demon to an individual. Sometimes clients will admit that they worshiped the devil or dabbled with quasi-satanic rituals when they were younger, thinking that it would fade away over the years. I believe that Satanism is selfish, naïve, and cruel—it also gives the illusion of power but is very fleeting. Most of all, it gives the worshipers the delusion that they are in control. No human ever controls or owns evil, despite what the entity may convince the individual to believe. Demons are parasites and will use the Satanist until they are no longer useful. We all know good always wins over evil anyway, right? Why bother meddling with the dark?

Is a poltergeist a demon?

From my experiences, I have found that most often, "poltergeist" cases are usually demonic in nature. Some theorists believe that a poltergeist is the result of a person's subconscious, or personal energy, manifesting the events and causing a haunting without their awareness—thus it seems that a foreign spirit is active in the home. (I no longer agree with this theory after years of experiencing supposed poltergeist cases.) However, I do believe that it is possible for a person's energy, such as an adolescent's, to *attract* an entity, which may lead to a haunting. It is extremely rare for a human spirit or personal energy to manifest such power and violence that poltergeist cases exhibit. If you are dealing with a poltergeist, it's best to perform a cleansing and remove the entity as soon as possible.

How can I perform a cleansing?

As my views and experiences have grown and evolved over time, so have my methods for house blessings. When I first started working with cleansings, I solely used white sage. From there, I incorporated olive oil, salt, holy water, and have experimented with various other herbs, plants, and incenses. In every room and area of the property I'm working in, I burn white sage (bathrooms, closets, basements, garages, etc.). I then sprinkle salt in every corner and draw a line of salt at each doorway and entrance into the home. Using the olive oil,

I anoint above every doorway and window. I finish with the holy water by sprinkling it in every area. During all of these steps I recite various prayers, mostly adlibbing from the heart, commanding the entities to leave in the name of God.

In the back of this book, I have included preparations and steps recommended for performing your own house blessing. House blessings and cleansing rituals can be as unique as the readers and it is important to find a method that works and is comfortable for you!

―――――

I invite you now to read about some of the severe cases I have encountered and to form your own opinions about the possibility of demonic hauntings.

CHAPTER 1
MY FIRST CONFRONTATION

The first time I confronted a demon, I was about seventeen years old. I had been dating eighteen-year-old Jack for several weeks when I began to notice the dysfunction in his family and the overall darkness that surrounded the house. Previously a happy and loving family, they now constantly fought and began to isolate themselves. Kevin, the father, slipped into alcoholism; the young adopted daughter, Hailey, began displaying a violent streak; and the youngest brother, Nate, attempted suicide twice in one night. As my relationship with Jack progressed, I was not surprised to find out the history of their home.

The family's brand-new house was built on the land that surrounded the old sanitorium in Howell, Michigan. Many people had died there from tuberculosis throughout the years. I believe land is imprinted with the energy of events and people—essentially a scar or memory is left on the earth that resonates throughout time unless properly cleansed. I have also observed that locations where mass amounts of death or despair occurred commonly attract demonic entities, as they feed off the negative energy. In retrospect, I firmly believe that the ground on which Jack's home was built on was inhabited by something evil stemming from the old sanitorium.

Jack would have unpredictable mood swings, worse than any adolescent I had seen. Despite being eighteen years old, his behavior was uncharacteristic for his age, and I had a hard time understanding where this originated.

His mother and I began to notice how his eyes would actually *change* during his angry tirades. I found this to be quite odd and unsettling. His normally calm and soothing hazel eyes would burn with an intense green. His pupils would darken and widen as if his consciousness had slipped into an altered state. Foul and strange obscenities would spew from his mouth during an argument. He would only resume his respect towards me after I threatened to leave.

One day I did leave.

After screaming that I was a "stupid fucking bitch!" I grabbed my purse and left the house. Jack tore through the house after me and proceeded to chase me in his Jeep. He was swerving through traffic and cutting off other drivers just to gain distance behind me. I finally pulled over, fearing that his asinine driving would injure someone else.

When Jack approached me this time, his demeanor had changed. "Look, forget whatever it was that I said. I didn't mean to hurt you ... " Jack continued with his explanation as if he had no recollection of the outrageous things he had said during the argument. His eyes looked normal again. I knew he was being greatly influenced by whatever entity resided in his home.

Most readers would say to themselves, "Just leave him and break up!" and I agree with you—that would have been a better idea, but I was determined to fight for Jack out of love and faith. I was still pretty young then and it didn't seem that crazy of an idea at the time. It should be noted that adolescent's frontal lobes are not fully developed, which leads them to make poor decisions and not fully think things through. That's my excuse. Through my rose-tinted glasses I continued to see Jack. Then even more curious events began to happen.

When I spent time at their house, Jack's sister Hailey would always cling to me as if I were some safety zone. Soon she started telling me about the weird tapping she heard on her window at night. I thought trees would logically be the cause for the rapping sound, but her room was on the second floor and not in proximity to any trees. She also mentioned how cold it was in her room and that she was scared to be alone there. I realized this was the reason she still slept in her parents' bedroom at the maturing age of nine years old.

The family's Golden Retriever Johnny would urinate and defecate all over the basement for no reason and seemed to hate being alone in the house. Despite all these strange incidents, when I discussed the possibility of ghosts, the family would scoff as if the paranormal realm was some figment of my imagination.

Aside from the worsening mood swings and habitual lying, Jack eventually started experiencing something even darker that he couldn't explain. He would have nightmares and awaken to show me foreign hand marks and fingerprints around his arms. One person alone couldn't replicate these with their own hands. I became more worried and determined to find a solution.

I began researching negative hauntings and how to remove them but was unsure if this was just a "ghost" or something darker. As a personal experiment, I brought a small bottle of holy water with me one day and left it in the passenger's seat of the car while I visited inside the house. The family had recently purchased a new vehicle and had several of their cars parked in the driveway. Amazingly, after being inside the house for only a few minutes, *all* of the car alarms began going off—including my own! I leaned over the kitchen window and saw my car's lights blinking and the horn sounding off. My car keys were resting in my purse on the kitchen table—no one had touched them. I didn't mention to the family that I had brought holy water and it was sitting in my car.

Jack's mother dismissed it as just a technical problem with the new car and turned off the alarms. However, it kept repeating. This happened several times and the family denied it as anything out of the ordinary.

I was baffled and now convinced that something darker was residing in their home. The sacrilegious reaction to the holy water verified my suspicions.

One evening at Jack's house, I was suddenly awakened with sheer terror. Jack's bedroom was located in the basement next to the bedroom of his older brother, Lenny. They both reported hearing the toilet seat down the hall slamming in the middle of some nights, along with an overall feeling of uneasiness. Needless to say, I wasn't a fan of sleeping down there. The unfinished basement proved to be very creepy. All I remember that particular evening was being engulfed with fear and drenched in sweat—no nightmare had ever made me feel that frightened. I felt the presence of pure evil in the room with me and I will never forget that sensation.

I looked over at Mick, Jack's pet red-tailed boa, and she was coiled up in the striking position while staring at something in the corner of the room—exactly where I sensed the presence. The snake's heat lamp cast an eerie red glow upon the room that made it feel even more sinister. My heart and mind raced as I glanced around the room, looking for an explanation for why I woke up. But in the back of my mind I knew why. I felt the distinct emotions of hatred and rage turned towards me; whatever was in that room despised me and wanted me to know.

I tried to gently wake up Jack but to no avail. Finally, I resorted to shaking Jack awake, but he lay there asleep, seemingly dead, for over eight or ten minutes. I later discovered that this phenomenon is known as "psychic sleep," in which it is almost impossible to wake the individual. My feeling of panic was so high I felt like I was being chased by a serial killer. *"Come on! Wake up, please!"* I whimpered to Jack.

I was being engaged by something dark and evil. The presence of evil is the most disturbing experience one could ever encounter and I don't think I could ever thoroughly explain the terrible feelings and energy that were present in that room. I was nearly in hysterics when Jack finally woke up.

Ashamed of how afraid I was, I sheepishly asked Jack for a glass of water upstairs. I never mentioned what I had just experienced.

Once we returned to the room with the water, I noticed that all the animals seemed to be uncomfortable. The cat refused to enter the room and kept meowing at us as if we were insane to even be in the same vicinity as the "thing." I lay back down and closed my eyes, mentally trying to block out the entity. I envisioned a white light surrounding me and I prayed. Eventually, we were able to fall asleep again.

I tried not to acknowledge the being whenever I visited Jack's home. I continued to envision white light surrounding me whenever I went over, and I tried to create a mental brick wall between the demon and myself. I hadn't figured out a plan to get rid of it quite yet and needed more time.

Another night we were at my house, cuddling after watching *The Exorcism of Emily Rose*, when we both witnessed a black light anomaly, or "orb," shoot out of the carpet and into the closet of my bedroom. The dark ball was larger than the size of a bumblebee and made no sound.

We commented on how strange it was but tried to brush it off. But we couldn't let it go and started to investigate. We didn't find any insects. There was nothing to be found inside of the closet. We couldn't find any reasonable explanation.

The entity seemed to follow Jack and was now apparently visiting my home, which made me very uneasy. That entity was not welcome in my house and I felt violated that it started to assemble "visits."

A few days later Jack was driving his Jeep Wrangler and saw flashes of black, brown, and yellow lights mysteriously flickering in the backseat of the car. He pulled over only to discover nothing out of place and no explanation for the lights. Later that evening, he lost control of his steering and brakes, as if some unseen force were controlling the car. My father, an automotive engineer and inventor, examined the car and stated that nothing was wrong with the steering or braking.

That night Jack emotionally broke down at a party we were at and explained that he wasn't happy, that something wasn't right with him anymore and he wanted help. This was the final straw that drove me to confronting whatever darkness hid within the house. It was affecting his sanity, emotions, and ability to function on a daily basis—something had to be done.

I had read about house cleansings and how to remove demonic entities, but I wasn't filled with the confidence I would have *really* appreciated at that time. I gathered my supplies, told my mother of my mission, and reluctantly left for Jack's house. My mother insisted that she could help, but I wanted to fight off the evil entity by myself; it would look strange if the family returned home and discovered both my mother and I there doing God-only-knows-what in their house.

The new home would be empty that night; Jack was still at the party where he had his meltdown—it was a perfect opportunity to bless the house without any interference from the family.

Jack's home was located about a thirty-minute drive from my parents' residence. As I drove, I tried to mentally prepare myself. The entire way there I repeated the Lord's Prayer over and over again, each time with more conviction, *"Our Father who art in heaven, hallowed be thy name ..."* I do not recollect most of the drive there, but it was intense as I tried to motivate myself with courage and not fear.

I pulled into the subdivision, seemingly with tunnel vision of my only goal in mind: to cast out the demon. I entered the home with my smudging supplies in hand. I could actually feel the entity waiting for me in the house, almost mocking my existence and my intentions of getting rid of it. I felt like a mongoose dancing with a cobra, waiting for the right time to strike; we were watching each other's movements.

And so the cleansing began. I worked my way through the dark house, burning the white sage. Oddly enough, much of the cleansing was also a blur, as if I blacked out during the process and Great Spirit had taken over. However, I do recall heading into the basement and sensing the entity's thick presence amongst the smoldering sage. The air was heavier and dense; I felt the pressure weighing down on my chest and the sides of my head. It almost felt as if a vice grip had been placed on my temples. I could feel that the basement was where the entity liked to hide, especially in the utility room. This was the same room where their dog Johnny would repeatedly soil and now I understood why. I believe animals are very sensitive to unseen energies.

I made my way through each room in the basement, blessing and praying, then headed down the long hallway towards the notorious bathroom and utility room. Prior to the cleansing I was a bit unsure of my ability to remove this entity—I hadn't attended church in years, as I disliked the glitz and tainted side of religion, and yet I was attempting something very few priests participate in. *Was I worthy enough of God's help?* Despite my hesitation, I suddenly felt the presence of Great Spirit walking with me and protecting me as I made my way through Jack's home. As I cleansed the storage room, which was adjacent to the utility room, I could feel the tension rising.

The air was extremely cold and thick; it almost had an electric feel to it. I had cornered a very angry animal and I half-expected to hear hissing and growling. I had finally come face-to-face with the demon that was tormenting this family. It was not happy with my visitation. I proceeded to bless the outside of the room as if to create a barrier, and I continued to pray. I was running out of white sage to burn and hoped that the remaining amount would be enough to finish the blessing.

Clips from movies began flashing in my head. I was worried that objects and furniture would be thrown at me and my fear would win me over. One side of me wanted nothing more than to run away from the house, but my stronger and more compassionate side demanded that I stay there to fight off this entity.

I prayed even harder and dared to add a tone of conviction with each word. *"In the name of God, I command you to leave this house and family! I cast out any dark or evil spirits from this home, in God's name I pray. Amen!"* This continued for several minutes longer until I felt the presence start to weaken. It felt like a bright sun was breaking through a thick fog. Darkness was relinquishing its grasp. I pressed on with my prayers and willed the evil to leave.

I was unsure if the presence had truly left the home and held my breath. The nausea in my stomach slowly faded and I went back upstairs to gather my "witch doctor" supplies, fearing the family's criticism if they were to return home while I was still there. *I just wanted to help them before things got worse.*

Jack came home later that evening and I worried the entity would come back full force and retaliate, something that I had read about in numerous books. However, I was pleasantly surprised to find out that Jack finally got a good night's sleep and nothing out of the norm happened. I was delighted that the cleansing provided him with some sense of relief and only prayed that it would last.

For many months the demon didn't make its occupancy known and the family seemed to return to normal. Eventually, Jack and I went our separate ways after about a yearlong relationship and I wondered if the demon remained attached to the family. I never did follow up to ask.

It should be noted that dysfunctional families who do not address their issues are more likely to have a relapse with a demon—unless they take a proactive approach and really begin altering their lifestyles and relationships. As a healer, I can perform the cleansing and remove the spirits, but it is truly in the hands of the family to make sure they prevent any entity from having a foothold with which to stay attached to them. For example, if a demon is affixed to a parent because of their alcoholism and they choose not to become sober, the demon is likely to stay with that person despite how powerful a house blessing is performed.

After the experience with Jack's family I began researching and trying to perfect the best techniques to use when cleansing a home from a demonic presence. I studied various cultures and religions and concentrated on the most potent methods.

I founded a paranormal group that year while at Central Michigan University and began receiving many requests for house cleansings. I started helping countless people and, through the power of Great Spirit, healing was brought into their lives.

In 2009 I relocated to Michigan State University and created the Michigan Paranormal Research Association (M.P.R.A.), which was followed by an overwhelming number of house blessing requests. Shortly after, I met and began dating my previous partner, Carl O'Toole. Mike Best, Carl's coworker, soon became a group member and accompanied us on several severe cases.

Because of the large number of cleansing requests, I could only respond to the most acute cases. The following chapters contain stories from my most disturbing and active cases.

CHAPTER 2

NOVI, MICHIGAN CASE

On April 17, 2010, in the early hours of the morning, I awoke from another nightmare. I had dreamt I was battling a demon; I found it hard to shake off the vivid and realistic qualities of the vision. In my dream I was praying and casting out the entity—a tall, dark, and faceless being—while speaking in Latin, even though I am unfamiliar with the language. The shadowy figure had a very strong presence and, although this altercation took place in a dream world, the tension and effort it took to ward off this spirit felt extremely real. I awoke exhausted and disturbed.

Later in the morning I checked my inbox and discovered an e-mail asking for help with a possible demonic case. The score was now five for five: every time I had a demonic nightmare I would shortly receive a request for help to fight a demon. *Was there some sort of correlation? Was I psychically tuning in to what I would soon encounter?* I already accepted the fact that my dream world was far from "normal"; I would have accurate death premonitions or encounter horrifically evil entities in my sleep.

Bad dreams were frequent for me ever since I had begun battling the demonic, something I also had to accept. I now slept with a Himalayan rock salt lamp on, as a soothing nightlight. Salt rock lamps are believed to promote a positive environment by releasing ions into the room, but I also believe it keeps the darker things at bay.

The request for help I received on this particular occasion was from a woman named Betsy. She claimed that her son Bryan had been physically thrown across the room by an evil presence the same morning she contacted me. I immediately called Betsy and talked with her about the experiences, trying to figure out when and why this entity had entered their lives. Betsy had a sense of urgency in her voice that I knew was genuine.

Out of all the cases we had taken over the years, only two individuals had questionable stories and a possibility of mental illness—Betsy was very earnest in her story and I could tell she wasn't being deceitful or just looking for excitement. I wanted to help protect her and her family from whatever it was they were experiencing. Although I was scurrying around with school and homework, I found this case to be particularly important and began scheduling a time for when we could visit.

Betsy and I discussed possible origins of the haunting. Betsy felt it might have been linked to the old farmhouse they had previously lived in. Carl's coworker, Michael Best, had been on several investigations with us before and I truly appreciated his rock-solid and reliable demeanor—he wasn't squeamish with the demonic. He was also someone who was serious about the client's well-being; he wasn't just seeking thrills through an investigation. I asked for him to join us on this cleansing.

We scheduled a meeting with Betsy and her family for a few days later—April 23, 2010.

Carl, Mike, and I all piled into the car and made the drive down to Novi, Michigan. It wasn't unusual for us to sometimes experience weird physical and psychic symptoms that foreshadowed the visit. Surprisingly, *all three of us* began experiencing a headache before arriving at the house. In the back of my mind I felt we were "picking up" on the entity that awaited us at Betsy's home.

We pulled into the neighborhood and mentally prepared ourselves by blocking out any negativity. Betsy's family lived in a friendly community surrounding the Novi area. There were lots of cars on the street and people were walking around; we then realized that it was prom night for many of the high school students in the neighborhood.

We prayed in the car together, huddled in like a bunch of football players ready to take on the opponent. *"God, please surround us with your protection and white light. Help us deliver this family from the evil they are experiencing and do not let anyone be harmed and do not let anything follow us. Thank you. Amen."*

As we approached the house I noticed that there were several students outside watching us, interested in what we were doing. I always prided our group on being very discrete; we never arrived in a large van with lettering on the side that screams, "We'll kick your ghost's butt!" Little did I know that the kids already knew exactly why we were visiting Betsy's house and a lot of the neighbors were fascinated with our paranormal endeavors. I smiled at them and followed the steps up to the house.

Two large dogs confronted us at the door, barking and growling with their hackles standing rigid. I absolutely love dogs, and all animals for that matter, but I felt uncomfortable with this pair being so upset and aggressive. We commonly see animals that are very distressed and frightened when co-habiting in a house with a demonic spirit. Sometimes I feel that the demonic can influence the animal's behavior as well. Thankfully, after our cleansings, the pets often return to normal and become very friendly and relaxed towards us.

I asked the man behind the screen door if Betsy was there.

"Yeah, come on in." The man moved away from the entrance and welcomed us inside the house while he carted the two dogs away into the backyard. The metal screen door had chew holes ripped through it from the dogs.

In almost every case I can immediately sense the dark presence in the house as soon as I walk in or prior to entering the home. I feel heaviness on my chest, pressure on my head, and sometimes my hearing begins to waver. The atmosphere seems dark and oppressed, as if lots of misery and depression resides there. The air is usually thicker and sometimes proves harder to breathe. On occasion, I also get the sensation of feeling "dirtier."

In the case of Betsy's family, the piles of clothes and clutter in the bedrooms added to the oppressed feeling. Many demonic cases involve clients that participate in "hoarding" or unorganized practices, although Betsy's family members were not hoarders. Keeping a clean home not only allows the energy to *flow* in a house more freely (i.e., feng shui), but your personal energy or aura is also cleaner and more functional. Many clients also tend to keep their houses extremely dark and don't allow sunshine to enter their homes. There is a lot of power and positivity that radiates through natural light, so it's important to integrate it inside your home by keeping your curtains open. The demonic seem to hate the light.

The sun fought to seep through the window treatments in Betsy's dimly lit house. I asked where I could place my supply bag and began pulling out my notepad and pen to take notes. The family nervously talked amongst themselves. I asked where they would like to meet to discuss things. The three of us soon settled into the living room with the family. I knew they were uneasy and understandably so—how terrifying it must have been to be plagued by such a malevolent force.

I explained our backgrounds, what I specialized in and how many families we had helped. This seemed to make them more at ease. I think it's very important to have a personal connection with each client and to relate to them as friends and family, not as some lab rat or opportunity for excitement.

I explained that we dealt with a lot of cases in which the haunting was severe or physical. I asked if they were comfortable with us talking with them for a while to pinpoint some things and then we would move on to performing a cleansing for them.

They all nodded in confirmation, even though I could tell they weren't entirely sure how the process went. The family introduced themselves and I sensed they were a loving group with a strong bond—something that would help them greatly in a battle against the dark. I listened to their introductions, each taking turns: Collin, Betsy, John, Sarah, and ending at the corner of the room with Bryan.

Bryan was the son who had been thrown across the room the day Betsy had contacted me. As the oldest son, he was nineteen years old, six feet two inches tall, and weighed about 300 pounds. He was not a lightweight and clearly could not be easily thrown. Although it was hard to visualize Bryan being lifted up and tossed by the entity, I believed the family and their accounts. Several family members witnessed the event and were horrified, each solemnly testifying to the incident. They said that Bryan had been standing, talking to his mother, when suddenly an unseen force lifted Bryan up from the floor and propelled him backwards a considerable distance.

Betsy expressed that she was finally fed up with the severe haunting they were dealing with and began searching for paranormal investigation groups. After skimming through different Google searches she stumbled upon the Michigan Paranormal Research Association (M.P.R.A.). What drew her to us was that we offered "solutions to hauntings," although she didn't know what that might exactly entail. She was skeptical but was desperate enough to try almost anything to bring her family peace and protection—the entity had been following them for over ten years and counting.

The family began sharing their experiences, trying to categorize a timeline of events. I was taking notes, trying to piece the puzzle together to figure out what attracted the entity to them. Once I discovered why the demon was welcomed in or drawn to an individual or family, it was easier for me to remove the haunting. And so as Betsy's family talked, a very impressive and long history of paranormal events unfolded before me.

The father, John, shared the history of the haunting, "We used to live in an old farmhouse outside of town before we moved in to this trailer. The previous owner's husband was a real violent son of a bitch. I swear if you dug into the basement dirt you would probably find bodies down there. He was suspected of killing hippie women or something and was always in trouble with his alcoholism. He also used to abuse the mother-in-law that lived there with him," John explained. "He was just a drunk hillbilly, but finally he died one day. Took him forever to die though! Karma served him right! He was T-boned by another car and it took him over twenty painful hours to kick the can!"

I was not sure how John knew these details about the previous owner, but it seemed they knew the family well. *Perhaps they were related.* After the man's death, Betsy's family moved into the farmhouse and they began to experience strange events. Disfigured faces would appear in the kitchen window at night, the family would witness a "cat-size" black shadow that would crawl along the floorboards and ceiling, a colonial girl was seen in the closet wearing a traditional dress, and Betsy would overhear the phantom conversation between two unseen men in the living room. It was very overwhelming for the family, but they continued to live there and attempted to ignore the spirits until they were confronted.

One day Bryan ventured into the back shed, looking for a shovel, when one of the old shed windows slammed shut on its own accord. Bryan heard movement behind him as though something was trying to ambush him inside the enclosure. Bryan made for the door and quickly stood underneath a nearby tree. He looked around and saw no animals that could have logically made the sounds, but Bryan knew in the back of his mind what the source of the disturbance was—the entity.

Bryan was scared but felt the need to stand his ground. After slowing his breathing a bit, he acknowledged the spirit out loud, "Well, if you're so tough, show me what else you can do …" Before finishing his sentence and challenging the entity, a large tree limb snapped in half directly above him. Stunned, Bryan left the shovel and hurried inside the house. The mangled limb belonged to a living and healthy tree. I could not provide a rational explanation for how this incident was possible.

The fear in Bryan's eyes spoke volumes to me and I felt he was being honest about this story. Needless to say, Bryan would never go outside near the shed unless his brother accompanied him. He learned from that experience to never challenge or antagonize an entity. Thankfully, the incident didn't leave Bryan physically hurt, but he was definitely shaken up.

Bryan continued to explain that at night someone could be heard down in the basement tinkering away on something. Whoever heard the sounds would then realize they were home alone or that everyone was upstairs already. He theorized that it was the previous owner because he used to work on projects in the basement.

Sometimes drawers would open on their own accord, sounds of metal—nails and washers—could be heard moving around. They also heard pounding and hammering. The basement was anything but vacant.

While all of these odd occurrences were taking place, John, the father, wasn't experiencing anything strange. It's not uncommon for only a few family members to encounter a severe haunting and the other spouse or member to witness nothing. I call this "singular isolation." This phenomenon will break down the family trust and bond, soon causing arguments and a negative atmosphere that dark energies thrive off of. John assumed the children were creating stories to receive attention and that his wife was playing into their games. *There is always a rational explanation for everything,* he thought to himself. However, he would soon witness the unexplainable.

After enduring nearly nine years of disturbances in the farmhouse, and with their finances dwindling, the family moved. Following about a month of living in their new home, things began to happen again. The family's hope sunk—they thought a haunting could only manifest at one house, and upon moving, they hoped it would be over with. They soon realized it had followed them to their latest home.

I asked Betsy if she thought this was the same entity or spirit(s) from the farmhouse or if it was an entirely separate haunting. "I think it might be the same spirit. We started seeing that black blob or shadow again, which was identical to the one in the farmhouse."

I explained to Betsy that many families experiencing a demonic haunting assume that they can escape by moving and relocating to a new home; however, they are disheartened to find the entity is attached to them and follows them to their new house. I assured her that in order to get rid of a demonic entity, it must be removed—you cannot hide from it as it will prove to be pointless more often than not. As with any issue in life, you must confront your problems and not run from them, only then can you begin to take back control of your life. Betsy and her family seemed ready to finally rid themselves of this entity, once and for all.

Interestingly enough, almost all of the paranormal incidents only occurred on the children's side of the trailer. Betsy did witness unexplainable events in the children's area so she knew the children weren't fabricating anything. It didn't matter what time of day or night, there was seemingly always activity. A lot of our cases would have the client waking up nightly at around 3:00 a.m. or in the wee hours of the morning to experience the haunting, however, for Betsy's family, some of the most violent episodes happened during the daytime.

The same week that Bryan was lifted off the floor, Bryan's best friend Jeff had been visiting the house one day at about eleven or noon. He was punched in the stomach so hard the wind was knocked out of him. They found old skeleton keys in their new home that seemed to belong to the farmhouse. Soon a pile accumulated.

The family relayed their stories to me in almost an immune tone, as if they had experienced so much terror they no longer showed emotions—it was their new normal. I would soon find out why the entire family was emotionally shut down and stonewalled.

I felt that the dark entity lurking inside the home likely influenced the previous owner of the farmhouse and then attached itself to Betsy's family once they moved in, but I wanted to check other possible sources. I began asking about the psychological and physical health of the family to see if some incident happened that enticed the demonic force. "Can you think of any problems you've experienced with substance abuse, alcoholism, sexual assault, depression, domestic violence, and so on?" After a long pause, the father, John, quietly stated that everyone in the family, aside from the youngest son, Collin, had been sexually or physically assaulted at some point in their lives. My heart sank and I told the family that I appreciated them sharing this with us, as painful as it might be to discuss. I discovered that they had not received counseling for their past traumas and I considered the abuse as a possible entryway for the demonic as well. The phrase *"The demonic prey on the weak and the ill"* has always stuck in my mind and is an accurate explanation for most of my cases. This entity was preying on victims.

"My grandpa used to beat the living shit out of me and assaulted me when I was little," John said. "I would try to defend myself, but I was too small. One day I was bigger than him, I grew up, and finally fought back." John had tears in his eyes but shared his story with a sense of dignity. Betsy squeezed his hand to reassure and comfort him. This family clearly had been to hell and back.

Betsy spoke up and began sharing her past as well. Betsy's mother abandoned her in California when she was about fourteen years old, taking Betsy's siblings and leaving Betsy to fend for herself. She got a job and enrolled in a self-defense class because Betsy was terrified that her trailer would be broken into and she wouldn't be able to defend herself. Despite Betsy's best efforts at a normal life, she soon battled a drug addiction, was sexually abused, and was swallowed by darkness and depression. Thankfully, years later she would recover and start a beautiful family of her own. She was a strong woman and knew the hardships of life but overcame them. Now the paranormal realm was biting at her heels. Betsy also shared that she had gone through several recent surgeries, lost her job, and that the family's health, finances, and happiness were starting to deteriorate, all of which were very characteristic of a demonic haunting. They filed for bankruptcy.

John and Betsy then moved on to explain Bryan's history. "When Bryan was little, his best friend's parents used to force him and his friend into performing theatrical plays, but the plays were sexual and perverse in nature. The parents would make them touch each other and do other horrible things. But, through all of that they still remained best friends for a long time." Betsy paused to collect herself. By the time they wanted to press charges, it had been over seven years and the police said it was too long ago for them to do anything about it or to charge the parents.

I couldn't help but feel anger and sadness for Bryan. I really wanted him to experience that feeling of justice being served and that karma had paid forward his friend's parents' behavior, but there wasn't anything I could do. Betsy explained, "We felt terrible when we found out. We had no idea that his friend's parents were doing that. No idea."

I tried my best at reassuring Bryan, apologizing that such a traumatic thing had happened to him. I gave Bryan my deepest condolences and reminded him that it was not his fault. There are some really ugly people in this world. I was really proud of Bryan for wanting to press charges and coming forward about his experiences; that takes a lot of strength and courage. I explained to Bryan that I lacked that same courage to press charges after I was assaulted in high school, and that he should be proud for pursuing justice.

There was so much pain in this house that I wanted to just sit and sob for the family. I could feel their emotions and pain, so much so that at some points it became overwhelming for me; my eyes welled up and I had to choke back full tears while hearing their stories of suffering. The string of bad events and darkness in their lives could have easily attracted a demonic feature—*perhaps there were multiple reasons for this haunting.*

The family continued with Bryan's history of paranormal encounters. They amazed me with their strength and love.

Ever since Bryan was little he had experienced paranormal events. He described seeing "rain people," which sounded very similar to silhouettes of ghosts. They were very foggy in appearance and Bryan remembered that it almost looked like rain. He stated that you could "kind of see through them." As Bryan got older he began having increasingly intense encounters with the paranormal. After the family moved into their new trailer, Bryan even considered that he might be going crazy, losing his sanity. Both he and his father recalled a time when Bryan was tormented for three full days—every body of water appeared to be thick, red blood. Whenever Bryan or his loved ones spoke, it sounded like wailing and thousands of tormented souls to Bryan.

The family was baffled. Betsy took Bryan to have a psychological evaluation and found out that he was not suffering from any mental illness like schizophrenia, or any other catalytic disease associated with hallucinations. There was no valid medical explanation for what Bryan was experiencing. He would have uncontrollable bursts of anger—sheer rage—and he started to isolate himself more. Bryan would experience strange things on a daily basis and the family would experience events once a week or so. Things were escalating in the household.

Carl, Mike, and I asked if we could speak with Bryan separately outside as it seemed that Bryan was being targeted the most. We went around the corner of the house and began talking. I told Brian that I wanted to get his perspective on things and ask a few more personal questions in private so he didn't feel embarrassed or pressured. "Do you ever black out after you get really angry or do you forget about things you've said and done during these outbursts?"

Bryan looked concerned, "Yeah, sometimes I don't remember any of it or I get really angry for no reason at all. What does that mean?" Bryan asked. I feared that perhaps Bryan was experiencing demonic oppression to the point that it might lead to actual possession. Possession is extremely rare but Bryan was beginning to show some signs of being heavily influenced—losing control of his body and emotions.

I questioned if Bryan was having any recurring nightmares or hearing any voices telling him to do harmful things.

"Actually, sometimes I hear some spirit talking to me. They'll say stuff like, 'Just kill yourself. You're worthless.' Things like that." Bryan was becoming anxious.

I then asked Bryan if the voice was male or female and if he heard it with his ears or inside his mind.

Bryan thought for a moment, "It was just a voice inside my head. I think it was male but almost unisex. I don't know. It's hard to tell." Bryan stood in front of us trying to recall the incidents. I suspected that the telepathic and extremely negative narration inside Bryan's mind were the actions of a demon.

In severe cases, a demon will sometimes begin a dialogue with the victim and start instructing them to do harmful things to hurt others or themselves. Usually the client won't realize or comprehend that this is a foreign voice, and not their own conscience—they begin to believe that these comments are their own thoughts or don't question their source, and sometimes they follow through with the instructions. Many serial killers and murderers have mentioned that the "voices" told them to do it, in detail and with specific requests, and they are found to not have schizophrenia or split personality disorder.

When I studied abnormal psychology, I wrote several long syntheses about the possible connection between assumed schizophrenia and demonic possession. I found some very interesting case studies that sometimes reminded me of clients I worked with, Bryan in particular.

"Bryan, since the demon might be focusing more on you, I want to make sure that we have you participate in the cleansing to help remove the entity. Is that okay with you?" I asked. Bryan agreed and we headed back to the house.

Bryan interrupted our return, "Hey, real quick before you go back inside. I didn't want to say this in front of everyone because Sarah would kill me." Sarah was Bryan's girlfriend that now lived with the family. "But Sarah was sexually assaulted, too, when she was little … I get so mad when I talk about this … When she was six years old one of her relatives used to cut her genitals with knifes and then would play with the wounds."

My stomach turned and I felt the pooling of saliva in my mouth from nausea. Visions of the assault flashed through my mind and I was sickened by the evil in some people. I still cry when I read this story to myself. I wasn't sure if I was having a psychic vision or if my imagination was generating the images. They were so disturbing: flashes of knives, blood, a scared little girl, and the close-up perverse evil smile of a man flickered in my mind. His stained teeth and facial overgrowth wrinkled in the form of a grin. He clearly enjoyed it. I was brought back to the present moment by the sound of Bryan's voice.

"She never will tell me which relative it was because she knows I would try to kill him. I would. I would fucking kill that bastard. I think I know who it is but I'm not sure." I immediately hugged Bryan and my eyes started to well up again, my face hot with so many emotions. I didn't know how this family made it through life with such terrible experiences, but they were still loving, good people. It was a miracle.

I apologized to Bryan—I was woefully sorry for what had happened to him, his family, and Sarah. There is no excuse for some people's behavior, and I think sometimes it's pure evil. Bryan was such a great person and I didn't want him to let those memories ever ruin him. He was so strong and brave and I knew he could make it through anything. He already made it through the worst and it was going to get better. I promised him.

Bryan pinched the bridge of his nose, trying to conceal his tears by wiping them away. We made our way back inside and joined the rest of the family in the living room again.

Shortly after getting settled back in the chair, we heard a knock on the door. Betsy reminded us that it was prom night and the girls were coming by to meet up with Jeff before heading out to dinner. Blue and green fabric began squeezing through the front door and the two girls soon appeared in their prom dresses.

They greeted us cheerfully. "Are you guys the ghost hunters? Anything cool happen yet? I love watching those shows!" They seemed ecstatic to talk about the paranormal but were soon close to running late for their dinner and headed back out the door with Jeff, who had briefly introduced himself as well. I giggled to myself because sometimes the paranormal enables you to have a twisted sense of humor. *Demons and prom night … sounds like the next bestseller or blockbuster movie*, I thought to myself. *Why hadn't anyone thought of this plot already?* I pursed my lips trying to hold back my smile and began "reviewing" the notes to get back in focus.

Betsy shut the door and returned to her seat. "While you guys were outside we remembered some other things that happened that you should know about."

She explained that one morning Bryan's girlfriend Sarah was taking a shower when she saw narrow fingers glide across the thin, white shower curtain, thinking Bryan was there. Sarah asked out loud if Bryan needed his razor. She unknowingly was alone in the bathroom while Bryan sat out in the living room. Hearing her talking, he made his way into the bathroom and asked her what she had said.

"I thought you were looking for your razor," Sarah reasoned.

Bryan was confused, "Why would I need my razor, I was just sitting watching TV. What do you mean you thought…" Before finishing his sentence Bryan had glanced over at the bathroom mirror and stood in horror. Condensation from the hot shower had collected on the mirror. The word "DIE" was smudged on the glass in capital letters.

Sarah became angry and questioned why Bryan would write such a thing on the mirror. It was the third time she had seen threatening words written there and the joke was no longer funny to her. The energy of the bathroom changed.

"Sarah, get out now!" Bryan fumbled to grab a towel for Sarah as more lettering began to appear on the mirror. "N." Sarah nearly fell out of the shower with soap still in her hair. "O." The invisible hand seemed to move extremely slow but with perseverance. "W." Bryan yelled for John to come to the bathroom as he helped Sarah leave the room. Most of the family gathered and quietly read the message out loud, "DIE NOW." Even more strange, the letters were written backwards.

Betsy immediately became very frustrated with Collin and Bryan. She demanded that they stop with their supposed antics as it had truly gotten out of control. This time Sarah confirmed that the message was *not* written by anyone in the family, as previously thought, but by something they couldn't see. Sarah finished washing her hair out in the kitchen sink and raced past the bathroom to get dressed in Bryan's room.

After the shower incident, everyone began sleeping together in the living room, giving up and surrendering their bedrooms and personal space to their invisible intruder. "It" was winning. Showers were only taken while another family member would supervise the bathroom, keeping the other person company in the now very-uncomfortable bathroom.

Things continued to get weirder and more terrifying. At night, dishes would fly out of the closed cupboards and smash all over the floor. This created a ritual of cleaning in the morning for Betsy, which proved to be difficult with her recent surgery and back injury. She was becoming more and more exhausted. The entity pressed on, determined to break down the family's will and happiness. It was persistent.

During these strange events, Bryan began finding mysterious scratch marks and burns across his body and on his limbs. For no apparent reason, Bryan would experience a hot burning sensation, only to find a new scratch mark or welt.

During our visit I asked Bryan's permission to document the scratches and I took several photographs. I tried to raise his spirits by joking around as if I were doing a professional photoshoot and he were a professional model. It was important to keep up good spirits even when the family was surrounded by darkness.

One night, Bryan sat up watching the Lion's football game. Bryan went into the kitchen and gathered some snacks. Upon returning to the room he noticed that his dad had stolen his seat in the recliner and was now watching the game. Bryan and his father sat for a while and Bryan made several comments to his dad about certain "crappy calls" that were made. John would quietly reply with "Yes."

Then John's loud truck pulled into the driveway. Bryan assumed his mother had run to the store, using John's truck. Bryan took his dishes to the sink and returned to the living room after cleaning his dishes. That's when he saw John walk in the front door with a few groceries in a plastic bag.

"Wait. What? You ... were just ... I mean, what are you doing? I was just talking to you." John asked Bryan what he was talking about and why he looked so startled. Bryan explained that he had just experienced an entire conversation with "John" while they watched the football game together. John hates sports and made a point of interrupting Bryan's story to make the fact known. John said, "I would never watch football or any sport on TV for that matter. Whatever he saw was not me!" The figure previously sitting in the chair was not Bryan's father, although it physically looked and sounded like John.

In demonic cases it's not uncommon for the family members' voices to be mimicked; however, this was the first case I had in which a physical manifestation interacted for a prolonged period of time.

After Bryan finished sharing this story with us, he went into his room and grabbed a drawing pad that he frequently used. He showed me the "weird triangle-shaped men" he used to draw when they lived in the farmhouse. They didn't mean anything to him until they moved into the trailer. One day, when Bryan and Collin were in the kitchen, they saw a shadow in the corner. It was shaped exactly like the figures Bryan had drawn.

Sarah had *also* witnessed this oddly shaped triangle figure a different time. She also saw a disfigured creature crawl into the corner of the living room. It sounded like a horror movie. Collin got excited while Sarah recalled the story and grabbed a video game from their television stand and pointed out a picture, "It looked something like this!" On the back of the case was a Gollum-like character with lanky limbs and a sinister face. He was excited to have a visual aid that looked similar.

How was this even possible? The paranormal world never fails to surprise me, but I listened with a skeptic's ear to see if I could rationalize any of the incidents. Then, right at that moment, one of the kitchen cabinets flew open on its own accord. It was as if the entity acknowledged our discussions about it, confirming that it was present.

My heart sped up and I looked around the room, scanning to see if one of their pets had opened the cupboard, but I found no logical answer. Carl, Mike, and I decided that we should begin the cleansing soon before any further events happened. It was time.

As we pulled out our blessing and smudging supplies, I could sense the entity in the house, anticipating our moves. The charcoal disk began sparking and popping on the stove and soon the earthy aroma of the white sage filled the air. We walked through each area of the house opening doors and closets. In each area, we recited a prayer:

"In the name of God, I command any unclean spirits and evil entities to leave this house immediately! Great Spirit, please bring this family happiness, good health, prosperity, and peace. Remove any negative influences and deliver them from any evils that are here. In your name I pray, Lord. Amen!"

We repeated our prayers during the entire ceremony while we blessed the house with olive oil and salt. I began sprinkling the holy water throughout the home with Bryan. As we moved from room to room I could feel the entity cowering and moving away from us as if it despised our efforts. Even though I had feared that Carl, Mike, or myself might be attacked, we pushed forward and commanded that the entity leave. *"In the name of Jesus Christ, I command you to leave this family and this home!"*

As we finished the house blessing, the air suddenly lightened and the house became brighter. The dogs stopped barking and the atmosphere grew peaceful. We gathered with the family to recite together a spiritual warfare prayer [included at the back of this book] as a final act of closing.

During the prayer, which takes several minutes to complete, Bryan began to get antsy. I soon realized the battle was not over.

I asked Betsy to lead the prayer, and we all repeated each segment after her. I saw Bryan hunch over and begin to sweat as he repeatedly aired out his shirt. Betsy rubbed Bryan's back to comfort him and I could see Bryan closing his eyes in order to further concentrate. He appeared to be extremely uncomfortable and was having difficulty in reciting the prayer with the rest of the family. He looked at me and I nodded at him as if to gesture that he should keep pressing forward with the prayer—something might have still been attached to him. Bryan regained his composure and continued with the prayer, despite his apparent discomfort. He writhed in pain.

In several case studies it was common for a client to become sick to their stomach during an exorcism, and I wondered if Bryan was experiencing a similar situation. I considered grabbing Bryan a wastebasket as insurance in case he felt the need to vomit.

We were on the final sentence of the prayer and Bryan had finally endured through it all. We all finished reciting the prayer and looked around the room. Silence pervaded as we all absorbed the happiness and positivity that filled the house. But best of all, love was present in the home and it felt so warm and beautiful. I felt like a small child wrapped in a mother's blanket of security. Absolute peace.

"I thought I was going to throw up!" Bryan exclaimed.

I asked how everyone felt and if anyone could feel the difference in the home. It was a drastically different house than when we first arrived. I felt that great things were now on the horizon for the family and they could return to a normal life.

"It feels lighter..." Betsy stated in an almost skeptical tone. But after a few minutes she said, "That is amazing! Thank you so much for coming and helping us."

She asked how much she owed us. After performing numerous house cleansings across the state I began to lose money and only asked that our clients donate an amount they were comfortable with to cover the travel costs and supplies. But Betsy's family was clearly in a financial bind. I told Betsy that they owed us nothing—I wanted to do this one "pro bono" for the family and prayed they would be on the road to recovery. Betsy and John were touched by my offer and Betsy began to tear up.

Betsy gave me a big hug. I could feel Betsy's tension and sorrows leave her and tears formed in my eyes. She was a beautiful soul despite all of the struggles and pain her family had experienced. Betsy gave me a very sincere and grateful look and nodded her head.

We all exchanged hugs and our goodbyes as Carl, Mike, and I packed up our belongings. We came in to their home as strangers but quickly bonded with the family through such a spiritual experience. I gave the family instructions to start organizing their rooms so they could begin sleeping there again. "No more sleeping in the living room and no more supervised showers. This is your home now and you must act like it. Think of it as being part of the Witness Protection Program—your old life is no longer a part of you, and you have moved on," I explained. Betsy's family understood that they would have to conquer their fears of showering and sleeping alone, but realized it was much easier now that the entity had left. I asked for Betsy to call me if anything came up, if the activity returned, or if they needed something. Carl, Mike, and I made our way back to my car and finished with a closing prayer for the three of us in private.

I asked how Carl and Mike felt now that the blessing was finished.

"I feel awesome! I am ready to go to work now!" Mike exclaimed. We laughed because Mike wouldn't be returning to his job for several days, but we were happy he felt *that* great. *Another successful cleansing*, I thought to myself as we made the long drive back home.

I was delighted to receive an e-mail from Betsy the next day:

"Hi, Samantha! Everything was okay. Our son slept in his room and he said he slept like a baby. He was even alone in there for a while after dark and he said that he wasn't

creeped out or anything. Thank you so much, all of you, for helping us. I'll keep in touch and let you know how it's going."

The last I heard from Betsy, they were doing wonderful and their lives turned for the better. Their story has been featured on television and is quite remarkable. My heart still goes out to that family and I pray they continue to live a blessed life.

CHAPTER 3
GROSSE POINTE, MICHIGAN CASE
—POLTERGEIST

Jackie and Bob were in their mid-sixties and lived comfortably in a luxurious home off the shores of Grosse Pointe, Michigan. It was a beautiful sunny day as Carl and I took the hour and a half drive down there, trying to enjoy the road trip before partaking in spiritual warfare yet again. The lake sparkled and glistened, and I felt the presence of Great Spirit with us, reassuring that our endeavors would be successful that day. Spiritual warfare, while gratifying, is draining because it changes your entire life.

I was close to turning twenty-three years old at that time and spent my weekends battling the dark and helping others instead of going out and partying like most people my age were doing. I had outgrown the excessive nightly partying early on, and I was content with my lifestyle, as it filled me with happiness—and a few scares on occasion—but it was never boring. Although it wasn't a clear and concise "career," I felt I was fulfilling my life path and mission here on earth, whatever that may be.

I was ready to remove this entity from Jackie's home; the entire week leading up to the blessing was a hellish one for me (credit: obnoxious demon).

On September 29, 2011, Jackie had contacted me regarding a "poltergeist" she was experiencing. Throughout all my years of research I had genuinely believed in poltergeists. However, I didn't agree with the common theory behind poltergeists, which is that a person's subconscious or personal energy manifests the events and causes the haunting, thus it seems that a foreign spirit is active in the home, but essentially one person causes an entire haunting. That being said, I did believe that it was possible for a person's energy, such as an adolescent's, to *attract* an entity, which may lead to a haunting.

Eventually, this case and other case studies I had read about would entirely change my opinion on poltergeists.

"It took my feet out from under me while I was walking down a marble hallway in our house and caused me to fall flat on the marble face-first...fractured teeth, needed stitches, that was last week..." I read over Jackie's message and instantly felt that she might not be dealing with a poltergeist. Instead, I felt she was dealing with a demon. Jackie declared, "The crosses I put up don't work." She had also given the demon a name: IT. In many of the demonic cases I handled, the clients nicknamed the entity

"It." I had met many "Its," aside from the famous clown one. *Maybe in the future*...

I had spoken on the phone with Jackie for over an hour, reviewing all her experiences and history. She spoke very quickly and precisely, determined that she was not losing her mind and was, in fact, experiencing something paranormal. Jackie would sometimes go on a tangent about some of her encounters, forgetting that I *did* truly believe her and didn't need further convincing. I almost always gave clients the benefit of the doubt, knowing that providing a precautionary house cleansing wouldn't hurt the situation, even if there weren't a haunting. "Water materialized out of thin air on our kitchen stool, we found black tarlike goo in our shower, the toilet water would boil, it would howl and sing show tunes in the heating vents, scratch and bang on the walls, and other stuff like that." Jackie listed off a bizarre inventory of all the goings-on in the house. If our conversation had been overheard, I'm sure we would have both been institutionalized. Thankfully, I was in the privacy of my home and sat at my desk as I jotted down notes, listening to Jackie's accounts on the other end of the phone.

Several days after talking with Jackie, I was sitting at my desk, again replying to e-mails and inquiries about hauntings. As I was typing and staring at the computer screen, I heard a tornado siren blare. *Tornados in October?* I sat frozen and realized that this sound wasn't a siren and instead was originating from *inside* my house. "WooooOOOOOOPPPP!" The sound started from a lower note and ended at a high pitch; unlike any siren or alarm I had ever heard. The hairs on my neck and arms stood up as the feeling of the house changed. It was not a siren test.

What once was the peaceful, protected haven of my home was now invaded by a presence I had not encountered before. I shot out of my chair and stood in the living room, which opened up between the foyer, kitchen, and office. My heart sped quickly and I stood there for what seemed to be minutes, trying to slow my breathing and pulse. Nothing in my house made that sound and the sensation of it was completely alien. I felt a dark presence in my home. "In the name of God, I command you to leave this house! You are not allowed here! You are not going to stop Jackie and Bob from receiving help! Leave. Now!"

I looked at my snoring English Bulldogs as they sleepily stared at me. "Did you guys not hear that?" I asked them. My adrenaline was still surging and I tried calming myself down. Jack and Annie, despite being luxurious couch potatoes, are some of the most alert and aware guard dogs I have ever owned. Apparently, they had *not* heard this shrieking that echoed through the entire house. *How was that possible?* Was I losing my mind? In retrospect, I believe that they have been protected from experiencing anything dark as a result of my promise to Great Spirit, as mentioned in the introduction. I was grateful.

I began connecting the dots and realized the entity that visited my home was the same one that had been bothering Jackie and Bob. Only two days after talking with her, the entity felt threatened enough to make a visit at my house. I knew I was being challenged by the same presence because

Jackie had mentioned that she would hear a siren blaring through her house from the heating vents. This was the second time that an entity had visited me prior to a house cleansing in an effort to prevent me from helping the client.

I believe that these entities try intimidating me so that I will fear for my own safety and decline further help to the clients. However, I was determined and would not bow out of helping a person in need. I made the decision to not inform Jackie of the event, trying to keep her nerves calm until after our visit. I didn't want to fuel any panic in Jackie's mind until we could calmly talk about all the events together before the blessing.

In my opinion, episodes like this prove that demonic entities *can* simply teleport or relocate themselves based on whatever their agenda is and that they are *not* human spirits.

I sat at my desk trying to regain my composure and continued writing my e-mail. I wondered to myself how powerful of a demon we were working against, as there is some unwritten hierarchy of the dark. Some demons are more powerful than others, going out of their way to disturb you, and others will hide and cower. We still had an entire week until we would cleanse Jackie and Bob's home. I anticipated that it might prove to be a difficult week for Carl and me.

It was.

Each demonic case takes its toll. Many clients don't realize the effect their cases have on my personal life and that I commonly have to sacrifice my peace and happiness in order to reach enlightenment for the client. Often, Carl and I would become agitated with each other when a severe case was pending, as if the entity was trying to disrupt our lives—hoping we wouldn't be together by the time the blessing was due. Although our romantic involvement eventually ended, Carl and I were very aware of these entities and their effects on us, so we consciously reminded one another that a cleansing was approaching and we were probably being influenced by an entity. After we acknowledged that possibility and caught ourselves, we became stronger and the demon's efforts subsided. Prior to Carl's affair, I remember him telling me about a sexual dream he had involving someone who looked exactly like me. However, this doppelganger quickly turned sinister and proceeded to assault him. After our separation, he reported having paranormal experiences at his rental home and I have always wondered if the entity from chapter six had a role in the outcome. Again, these cases take a toll on anyone involved.

In the case of Jackie's demon, I was unable to sleep the entire week prior to the cleansing. I would repeatedly wake up at 3:00 a.m., knowing that I was being disturbed during the "unholy hour." It is thought that 3:00 a.m. is a mockery of the 3:00 p.m. "holy hour," when Christ was believed to have died upon the cross. Again, demons love to mock the holy trinity or anything sacred.

I lay there awake and alert. My eyes would inform me there were shadows in the corners that were darker than usual and the energy of my bedroom seemed to hold its breath. I would lie there trying to go back to sleep but my senses were wide awake, as if I sensed a predator nearby. The entity had already visited me and shrieked in my home, now it was causing me to lose sleep. *Every* consecutive hour I would awaken each night, and I was becoming very frustrated. I greatly needed some rest in preparation for the blessing.

This wasn't the demon's first time in keeping someone awake.

Jackie began noticing a darker presence in their house after she underwent a surgery a year prior at the University of Michigan hospital. Although unusual, this wasn't the first case in which an entity had followed a client home from a hospital. Being a Michigan State Spartan, I teased with Carl about how the University of Michigan's hospital was contaminated with demons and thus was at fault for Jackie's demise. "Wolverine demons … ugh! Is there anything worse? Demons already have large egos to begin with!" However, this was all in good fun and it is plausible that any hospital could harbor darker entities with the amount of death and sadness that surrounds these institutions.

The day of Jackie's surgery, her husband Bob arrived at the hospital to pick her up after the procedure. "I remember it was a full moon that night," Jackie recalled. On the way home from the hospital, Bob's demeanor completely changed and he became very resentful towards Jackie. "He told me to shut up and threatened to drop me off and make me walk my way back home. We were easily over an hour from our house." Through their thirty-six years of marriage, Bob had never been one to make such comments or be disrespectful towards Jackie. *Why was he behaving like this?* Jackie silently pondered.

Overwhelmed by the intensive surgery and medication, Jackie lulled off into a heavy sleep until they arrived home.

"The next day Bob was back to being Bob. I didn't mention the argument we had the night before in the car, because I was afraid I'd upset him again. I didn't ever want to see that side of him again."

Jackie's health began to rapidly decline after her surgery. She was bedridden for nearly four weeks, a condition that was unexpected by the doctors. Her hair began falling out and Jackie seemed to age more quickly. Before the procedure, Jackie was a healthy and robust woman. She would go running every day and frequently played tennis with her friends. It seemed as though her energy was being sucked out of her and fed to the entity. Towards the end of her time being bound in the bed, a strange knocking began. "First it started in the office room. I could hear it rapping away in there. I thought it might be the computer, and had someone come examine it but nothing was wrong. Then it began knocking on the windows and soon moved to the headboard. I was losing sleep and was being driven insane!"

Bob had not experienced anything abnormal and was never home during the events, leaving Jackie to feel very alone and questioning her own sanity. "I would mention this to Bob, but he just thought I was letting my imagination get the best of me. He hired so many technicians and fixer-upper guys to come look at our house."

One day Jackie heard a strange gurgling sound in their master bath. As she approached the bathroom, she was perplexed to find that the toilet water was bubbling and boiling in the toilet bowl. "Bob immediately called a plumber and he arrived a few short hours after our phone call." Jackie sat there explaining the incident to the plumber as he finished examining the toilet and plumbing lines.

As he placed the cover back on the toilet, he turned to her and calmly asked, "Well, do you think you have a poltergeist?" Jackie was surprised that a man of his profession would openly suggest such an idea. I quickly reminded her that plumbers and the paranormal seem to go hand in hand these days. "You remember the Roto-Rooter guys on T.V., right?" Jackie and I laughed.

She continued with her story, "I recall looking at the plumber and he arched his eyebrows at me as if he knew that I was already aware of the house being haunted."

"Maybe you should call a priest or bring in one of those ghost-buster groups? Maybe they can explain all of this and help you," he suggested while packing up his belongings.

Cue the Michigan Paranormal Research Association. And so we rode in on our white horse with shining armor. Instead of having a white horse, I had my white Ford Escape, but it proved to be a sturdy and valiant mobile. *"Turn right. Recalculating. Approaching destination. Recalculating."* Before leaving my house, TomTom, my GPS, knew the exact location of Jackie's home and how to get there, but upon nearing the destination, it no longer recalled its whereabouts—as if the GPS were on trial and now conveniently forgot its previous statements. The GPS seemed as if it were overcome by the demonic entity and was now giving us driving directions.

"Would you make up your mind! Damn it, TomTom!" I was tempted to throttle the GPS until it gave us more truthful directions. I glared at the device and Carl and I both laughed at our situation. It wasn't uncommon for our devices and communications to malfunction prior to a cleansing, as if the entity was making one final attempt to get rid of us.

After driving in circles, slowly closing in on Jackie's home, we finally spotted the correct driveway into the subdivision. I pulled into a very lavish labyrinth of beautiful homes, just across from the lakeshore of Lake St. Clair. I remember reading that some hauntings were closely situated next to a body of water or a river, and that the paranormal (or energy) can be conducted by water, thus leading to more intense or frequent hauntings of homes by water.

I parked the car, ready to finally confront this entity once and for all. Carl gathered my belongings and we walked up the front steps. The doorbell made a symphonic performance and I smiled at Carl. We had seen very impoverished families and those that were extremely wealthy, all of which were experiencing a severe haunting. The paranormal connects us all and completely disregards social class. It can happen to anyone.

Jackie seemed relieved by our presence and ushered us into the kitchen. I told her that she had a beautiful home.

"Oh, well, thank you," she said. "I wish it felt like home." Jackie seemed more annoyed than fearful of the entity, which I found to be very helpful. I want clients to be in control of their homes, to not fear the entity, and to have the ambition to reclaim their personal space when the time comes.

We asked if Bob was also home and if Jackie could have him join us. Carl explained that we needed everyone to be present during the cleansing and to discuss matters together as a group before we began the process.

Jackie seemed less than formal with Bob, as if she were calling in her obnoxious sibling. After watching Bob and Jackie interact I could tell that their marriage was strained and they seemed to be agitated by each other's presence. They loved each other but were content with their own separate lives. Jackie would repeatedly cut Bob off from speaking and their communication process was imbalanced. I tried to encourage Bob to continue with his thoughts and reminded them that they would have to take turns sharing their stories. It was important to get Bob's side of the story and to listen to his perspective as well.

Bob was a man of luxury. He thoroughly enjoyed his cigars and going down to the clubhouse to play cards with other gentlemen his age. After a while of sitting and talking with Jackie and Bob, he became concerned with the timeline of our visit. "How much longer will this take, do you think?" Bob asked as Jackie swatted at him from across the table.

"However long it takes, Bob!" She rebutted.

Bob explained that he was a devout Catholic and greatly believed in God. Jackie wasn't religious but shared the same faith in our Creator. I only ask that clients believe in a higher being in order for the blessings to be successful. They must ask this divine presence to come into their lives and help them remove any evil in their homes. If they don't believe in a higher power, I can never guarantee that the cleansing will work.

We continued our conversation and I asked them to share any mutual experiences in the house. The two of them recalled a time in which, finally, they together experienced something paranormal in the house. Bob had been getting dressed one morning when he smelled a terrible sulfuric odor. Sniffing around the room, he was finally led into the master bathroom and began searching for the culprit of the stench. To his surprise, Bob opened the shower door to discover an entire mess of black tarlike substance spread throughout the shower. "Again we called a plumber, but they provided us with no explanation."

Bob and Jackie had a very difficult time cleaning up the black slop and my dorky scientific Bill Nye side hoped that they had kept a sample of the substance, but to no avail. *How did entities manifest such a substance out of thin air? What was it composed of?*

Bob began to experience more personal incidents with the entity. In his second-floor bath, he witnessed a small fly turn into a large horsefly; it then harassed him. Bob was a very logical, left-brained, sensible man. Claiming that a small fly morphed into a giant horsefly and then assaulted him was something his conscience had a hard time accepting. Bob would share his strange experiences with Jackie, only to later withdraw the statements as if they had never happened or he had second-guessed himself. Many demonic cases include instances in which clients experience insects appearing out of nowhere in swarms, or clients are attacked, or infestations of various kinds begin (mice, flies, hornets, and so on).

More strange incidents occurred and the animals in the house seemed to become affected as well. Jackie was fond of taking in stray cats from the shelter, letting them seek refuge in their home. The cat food and toys were boundless and all felines were content, except for one. A few months before our appointment, Sasha the cat had suddenly become very ill, hiding under the bed for days, never wanting to leave the room. Soon the other cats became nervous and would often behave as if they were observing some unseen presence floating about the room and on the ceiling. Jackie would watch the cats as their eyes flickered with movement—unsure if she wanted to look and witness whatever they were watching.

I discussed with her the possibility that the entity was using her cat's energy or feeding off of them. Unfortunately, animal companions are easy prey for the demonic and it's important to protect them. I had seen cases before in which the family pets slowly began dying off without viable reasons from the veterinarian, or under strange circumstances. I didn't want the same thing to happen to Jackie's cats, as she loved them dearly.

Prior to our visit, Jackie had tried taking matters into her own hands. She said, "I started spraying every room, nook, and cranny in the house with vanilla spray, which did seem to calm IT down last spring, but as you know, it came back even stronger. The vanilla idea was a suggestion of someone from a paranormal internet site I had contacted at that time. Who knows if it's just a placebo or if it actually does anything."

I've never read about vanilla being effective, but I applauded Jackie's efforts and willingness to try almost anything.

Her eagerness to fight would save her home from the unwelcomed intruder.

After sitting and talking with Bob and Jackie for quite some time, Carl and I asked if we could begin with a tour of the house to identify the particularly "active" rooms. Bob retreated down into his basement office area and began puffing on a cigar. Although I can usually sense the additional tension and heaviness of the active rooms, I ask the client to identify them for me so I can spend additional time trying to clear out the negative energy in those locations. Depending on the entity, these rooms tend to feel unbalanced, electric, and disorienting—almost as if there were an energy shift present. It's quite an unusual sensation, although not an enlightening one. Most people feel uncomfortable in these areas, sometimes succumbing to nausea, headaches, and body pains.

I would be lying if I said it was a piece of cake to remain in those rooms while I cleansed them. I also request that the clients distinguish these areas because on occasion the entity will be moving and shifting around the house so that their presence can't be sensed during the "walk through" therefore making it harder to sense the active rooms.

The demonic are tricky in that they will avoid providing any evidence of their existence, at all costs. If proof is given that there is a demonic entity in a house, then the client usually is able to receive help—something that is loathed by the entity.

This is the reason I dislike the fact that many churches and exorcists require solid and undeniable proof of an evil presence before they consider offering assistance. Personal experiences are often ignored. It is almost impossible to document the demonic!

Jackie asked if we were going to perform a miniature investigation before the cleansing. I told her I prefer not to conduct formal investigations for demonic cases. I like to hit the demonic head-on. I don't want to give the entity time to observe and analyze me, allowing for it to drain my energy or attach itself, trying to detect any weaknesses so it can gain an advantage. I show up. I cast it out with the power of Spirit.

I understand the quest for outstanding evidence that paranormal investigators constantly search for, but demonic cases are not to be played with. If I had my druthers, all paranormal investigators wouldn't dabble with severe cases, and they especially would not investigate them. The priority as an investigator is to help the family, not to run a science experiment. By inspecting such cases, the investigators not only put themselves at risk but also the family and all those involved. It is better to nip it in the bud as early as possible and get straight to detaching the entity, much like a tick.

As we took the tour of Jackie's home, the cats scattered about the house like birds flocking to the trees and telephone wires in anticipation of a storm rolling in. I'm sure the cats could sense the contest that would shortly begin.

When we walked into the master bathroom, I became extremely dizzy and sick. Perhaps I was biased because I had already heard of Jackie's experiences there. The entire master bedroom seemed dark and dreary, as if an air vacuum gripped the space. Finding it difficult to breathe, I walked around the room and began opening the blinds, allowing sunlight to flow into the room. As always, natural sunlight works wonders. The air seemed more readily available and I gathered my intuitive impressions. I confirmed my suspicions: this was not a poltergeist. The energy in the room was malevolent and felt identical to other demonic cases. I told Jackie that we were ready to get started.

As we headed back towards the kitchen Jackie pointed out the long marble hallway where she had been assaulted by the demon. Underneath the beautiful exterior of the decorations, the fine Persian rugs, and the marble floor, there was a sinister darkness lurking. I stepped on to the marble and a fog clouded my head as a daydream began unfolding. In my mind's eye I saw Jackie's attack—it matched her description of the event.

Jackie had been out running that morning, as she was accustomed to, and sat in her kitchen enjoying a refreshing glass of water. She placed the empty glass in the dishwasher and decided that she would head upstairs to get changed. Jackie left the kitchen and walked down the marble hall towards the stairs. As she was moving, an "energy force" lifted Jackie off her feet and slammed her face directly into the floor. She heard the crack of her teeth against the solid marble and blood began to pool around her head. Bob heard her screams and immediately called for an ambulance, unsure of what had just happened. "It tripped me, Bob!" Jackie sobbed uncontrollably. She felt violated and scared—leaving questions in her mind of what else "It" was capable of.

Clips of this attack blipped through my mind as if my brain were a sonar radar picking up on psychic pinpoints. It was psychic confirmation for me that Jackie had really experienced such an attack.

Jackie had her top front teeth replaced and required stitches to repair some of the damage. She was not some elderly woman that just happened to fall and was quite frail; she was attacked. I stared at the marble, analyzing the room and the configuration of the flooring. I realized that it was unlikely for Jackie to trip between the hallway and kitchen because both of the floors were even and equal. There wasn't some bulky transitional piece waiting to hurt someone. I shuffled my feet over the area to see if it was slippery or if I could manage to trip myself—it would have been quite a task.

Jackie noticed my efforts and muttered, "Yeah, that's where it happened."

"I can't see how you just accidently tripped here," I assured her. I probably sounded like Captain Obvious to Jackie, but I wanted to rule out any logical reasons for her accident.

Carl and I laid out my supplies on the kitchen table. I asked Jackie to open some of the windows in each area of the house, including the front and back door. Carl lit the stovetop and placed the charcoal disc over the flame. It began sputtering and sparking in its familiar fashion. With all the tension present, it sometimes felt like the house could combust in a similar manner.

"I want you and Bob to sit here and focus on willing the entity to leave this house. Envision that you are taking back your home and visualize the darkness leaving. Command it out in the name of God and keep yourselves focused," I instructed Jackie as she went to gather Bob downstairs.

Bob soon emerged from his basement office ready to finally rid whatever was tormenting his wife. The haunting had primarily been one-sided and, although he had questioned the validity of Jackie's stories on occasion, he knew she was genuinely disturbed by the haunting. He was happy to cooperate in any way to remove it.

Bob shuffled across the room and quickly settled into his chair at the table. It seemed as though he had his game face on, which I was sure he'd frequently used during his card games with the boys. His bushy eyebrows narrowed and I half-expected him to give the coordinates to sink the battleship. Jackie and Bob were on board and ready to go.

"I cast out any darkness residing in this home in the name of God…" I began my routine of praying while smudging the room. Much of my praying is impromptu, which might seem controversial to those who follow strict religious methods. As long as it's in the name of God and I'm thorough in my requests and commands, it works. *"Lord, please remove any evil and negative entities in this house. Bring this family peace, prosperity, health, and happiness. In your name I pray."* On occasion I'll recite the Lord's Prayer just to be detailed; it brings comfort to many.

As we ascended up the stairs towards the bedrooms, the house began making unusual sounds in every direction. It was as if the structure were weakening under pressure. The demonic always like to make things dramatic. As in any good action movie, darkness doesn't give up without a fight. Suddenly, the abalone shell holding the charcoal grew increasingly hot, to the point where it was difficult to continue holding on to it. This was abnormal, but was something I had experienced before while cleansing another demonic case. If there is a way to distract me or prevent me from completing a cleansing, the demonic will try it (items go missing, phones start ringing, neighbors come over, doors won't open, and so on).

I was insistent on proceeding with the cleansing. I held on to the abalone shell tightly as the sweat on my hand helped diffuse the heat. Carl began teetering on a chair while trying to lift the door to the attic space. I wafted the white sage smoke up into the attic with my ceremonial feather and began throwing salt into the space as well. I made sure to let the smoke carry itself up and into the ventilation system as Jackie stated that much of her experiences involved hearing the entity howling and screaming through the vents. The smoke poured into the ducts and I was pleased.

We continued smudging throughout the entire home and were very thorough. When we were out in the garage, Jackie made an interesting request. She wanted us to smudge her Mercedes-Benz—a beautiful sporty coupe. I had silently eyeballed the car earlier during our walk-through. It was gorgeous.

"One day I was out driving last winter," she said, "and I had just purchased this car about a month or two before, when the brakes went out!" In the back of my mind I thought about the time when I was seventeen years old and dating Jack—his Jeep also started acting up and he lost control of his steering and braking for no reason. It was not uncommon with some demonic cases.

Jackie continued, "I tried slowing down, but the brake was stuck to the floor! The road was clear, no ice or anything, but I couldn't stop! I ended up sliding into a snowdrift that was melting and it slowed down the car. I immediately called Bob. He raised hell at the dealership and they found nothing wrong with the car."

I had a hard time envisioning a demon as a grease monkey, tinkering away on the car in one of those jumpsuits with a nametag reading "Earl," but this was the second time I had heard from a client about an entity taking control of a vehicle. Jackie opened up the doors and insisted that I sit in her car and smudge "the crap out of it."

It was a gorgeous car and I felt guilty about putting thick smoke into the interior, but Jackie wanted to make sure that she'd never have car troubles again—or at least car troubles caused by an entity. I recommended that she leave the doors open and allow the car to air out so it wouldn't leave a permanent odor. After we finished with Jackie's car, we returned inside the home and pressed on with our efforts.

The clicks, bangs, and groans continued throughout the home as we made our way through each room. The house wasn't old or creaky—I couldn't find a scientific reason for the sounds.

We entered the master bathroom and I began experiencing the same vertigo I had encountered earlier. It was hard for me to breathe and the dizziness started swirling about my mind. I continued with my prayers, hoping that I would never reach a point in which I could no longer continue a cleansing.

To this day, I have not had to stop my efforts during a blessing because of paranormal side effects and I am grateful.

As I prayed harder and commanded the entity to leave the home, the thickness and oppression began to dissipate. Slowly but surely. I thought about all the trouble this entity had caused in both Jackie's life and my own. It would be wonderful to finally have this demon cast out and to resume our "normal" lives.

I could feel the negative energy finally release its hold on the master suite and worked my way through the office. As I stood by the staircase I called down to Jackie to see if she wanted to "test" the bedroom to feel a difference in the atmosphere. Jackie slowly entered the room, as if she were expecting to be mugged.

Instead, she was delightfully surprised. "It's like there is actually air in here!" Jackie exclaimed.

I told her we would be done soon. I now felt it was safe to tell her of my experience with the strange siren sound in my house. "A few days after talking with you I heard an odd voice in my house. It sounded like, WooooOOOOOOPPPP!"

"Oh my Lord!" Jackie immediately reacted to the sound I mimicked. "That is *exactly* the sound I heard echoing through the heating vents!" She rubbed her arms as goose bumps chilled her body. Her genuine reaction of fear was mixed with disgust. She put her hands out in front of her as if to say *"Ugh! I don't need to hear anymore!"*; the sound had haunted her for quite some time.

"I just wanted to confirm that it was the identical sound. I figured it was the same entity from your house, but wanted to ask you just to make sure." In a way, it was relieving to receive validation from clients that I had experienced their entity visiting me. I wasn't crazy and there was no rational explanation for the event. I wished it was caught on an audio or video recording.

Although I rarely conduct formal investigations for demonic cases, occasionally I will leave a digital voice recorder running to document the client's interview. Sometimes I'm able to capture electronic voice phenomenon (EVP), but it's not common. Then again, I couldn't have predicted that the entity was going to visit my house and make a screeching sound. Like I said earlier, it's hard to document the demonic!

We finished our last round through the house with the holy water and returned to the kitchen with Jackie and Bob. We sat down and began reading the final warfare prayer together as a group. Bob led the prayer and we repeated after him. *"…I cover myself with the white light and protection of God. I claim the protection of the light for my family, my finances, my home, my spirit, soul, and body."* I could tell that Bob was excited to be nearing the end of the prayer, as the clubhouse was beckoning for his participation in a card game. I just hoped that he had honest intentions of getting rid of the entity.

I told them that, while it was a long prayer, it was thorough and would help a lot with verbally claiming back their rights and denouncing the entity's powers. I gave Jackie and Bob copies of the prayer for them to keep if anything should happen again. I also left some salt and white sage for them to use in case they felt that the home's energy was being compromised in the future.

Bob said his goodbyes and was on his way. Jackie turned to me and smiled, "Thank you again, for everything. I'll keep in touch and let you know how everything goes. I can feel that it is gone, though!" Jackie escorted us to the door and we said our goodbyes.

In the few short hours it takes to bless a home, I really bond with the families and individuals. I feel their pain, fear, and in the end, their happiness. It is an emotional rollercoaster but is well worth the fight.

I looked forward to finally getting more restful sleep again, as I had felt like a zombie the whole week. I climbed back into the car and the GPS no longer gave us any flack.

A few weeks later I was sad to hear that Sasha, the cat who had fallen ill after the entity arrived, had passed away. Sometimes as a final act, demons will claim the lives of innocent animals before they finally leave. I knew the cat was no longer suffering and was in a much better place. The vet lacked an explanation.

On the bright side, however, I was delighted to read that Jackie was ecstatic about the entity being gone:

"The evil spirit is now definitely no longer here. You got rid of it; I have not sensed it, and have not heard it since the day you and Carl were here. It's amazing, really; no more witches' coven siren songs from the vents, no more howls. Wow. Never had anything like that before. Sometimes I have to ask myself if this stuff is all in my imagination because it seems so outrageous. You have given all of the things I have

experienced, really all of my life, an explanation. Thank you."

I only heard from Jackie on a few other occasions. She asked if a light bulb that flickered in the living room and a tapping sound from the new computer was "It" making its return. I reassured her that when a demonic entity returns, they usually come back full force, as if they have had time to store up their energy and are now unleashing it upon the family. Since there were no signature events going on, such as the howling and screaming, I assured her that the light was probably an electrical issue and that computers do make anomalous sounds.

Jackie agreed the following week that it was truly gone and she was just nervous about it trying to return. I reminded her not to dwell on the past, to not think about the entity anymore, and to move on with her life. Since then, she has done just that.

A few years after the case, Jackie found video footage from her cell phone. While attempting to take a picture of her cat in the basement, she accidentally took a video. The short clip includes a mechanical shriek with muttering in the background. Both sounds were not heard at the time of recording but the cat clearly reacts to the disturbance. The cat in the video was Sasha. Jackie sent me the video for viewing and it served as validation for us both. It matched the shrieks we both heard separately in our homes.

Jackie and Bob are living happily in their home and I am happy to have helped them with the unknown.

CHAPTER 4

FLINT, MICHIGAN CASE

Whitney and David were a middle-aged couple with a seemingly healthy relationship. That year they had been renovating their 1930s home, trying to refinish the majority of the house themselves with the help of friends and family. Shortly after Whitney and David began their restoration, odd events and experiences began to unfold inside the house. Notably, the activity increased after they started tearing apart the old fireplace, which was located in the center of the home.

David had grown up in the house and both of his parents had passed away in the home many years back. The family had great aspirations for the house and looked forward to finishing the refurbishments once disposable income became more readily available. Until then, the renovations came to a standstill and the house was kept in disarray. Rubble, lumber, and drywall cluttered the kitchen and the disorder of the house was beginning to affect the family greatly.

It was September 3, 2010, and I sat cupping my mug of hot tea, feeling the warmth travel into my hands and arms—it helped counter the chills I got when reading Whitney's request for assistance.

"I happen to have a demon or something like it in our house. I have put a night-vision camera in the room at night and in the daytime and it messes with the camera a lot ... we hear something walking, and at times it is a heavy walk with claws clicking on the floor. It sounds like a Saint Bernard or something bigger ... We also have gone in the room at night and sat there and asked it questions and we didn't hear anything until we listened to the recorder. It answered us alright and not nicely! We also have a short, dark shadow that comes and goes ... So now I sleep with the light on! Now, even with the light on ... something I can't see starts growling in the corner! So after a few times of that I sleep on the couch downstairs. I hate not being comfortable in my own home and I don't know what to do. A few churches said they don't bless houses and don't know anyone who does! Do you have any advice for me? Anything would be appreciated. Thank you for your time."

Carl, Mike Best, and I sat there listening to Whitney and David in their home, trying to pull together a timeline of their experiences. It was our day off from work and school, being an observed holiday, but Whitney felt that a house blessing was desperately needed. We complied and spent our holiday fighting the dark side (not to be confused with the Darth Vader dark side).

It had been a colder-than-usual September morning and fall was slowly making its presence known. I had always admired how the seasons changed in Michigan and each year we were shown a fantastic display of colors in the leaves. I sat on Whitney's living room couch jotting down notes as the monotonous rhythm of the rain tempted me to sleep. The colder season, for some reason, had always correlated with an increase in paranormal activity, and especially a boom in house-blessing requests. Some believe the "veil" between our worlds is thinnest during the fall.

"It was like, as soon as we tore into the fireplace and began our demolition, our finances went to crap and the mood of the house changed entirely," David explained during our interview.

Although many would stipulate that the death of David's parents in the home was the origin of the haunting, I believe that most spirits cross over and do not remain to haunt a location. I explained to David that just because there was a death in a home did not mean there would be a haunting.

I assumed the renovations were the cause of the haunting. Numerous paranormal cases have been mysteriously linked to building renovations, as if the haunting is created once the building's features are altered. I think renovations may release energy that was imprinted inside the home, which may lead to spirit encounters. Then again, maybe the spirits were previously there and out of contempt for the renovations, they make their presence known. There are plenty of theories, and I have yet to settle upon one line of thought to explain renovation hauntings.

I initially thought that perhaps David and Whitney were experiencing a residual human haunting. But when I listened to their personal experiences, I changed my mind. This sounded like something darker. *Could a demonic haunting really result from a renovation? I thought renovations were only related to human spirit hauntings* ... There had to be more to the story that we were missing and I continued asking questions. Whitney and David sat across from us and began sharing their accounts.

One day while Whitney was using the computer, she witnessed a cowboy hat being thrown down the stairs by an unseen force. No one else was home and Whitney felt very uncomfortable. After inspecting the stairs and where the hat had previously been sitting, she concluded that it could not have fallen on its own accord. She later mentioned the event to David, but he was unsure in his mind if it was paranormal or something explainable. After speaking with Whitney, he shared with her that he had also experienced strange things while he was home alone but disregarded them, as many individuals do.

While David was gone at work, Whitney would often hear disembodied voices inside the house and shadows would move about the rooms. Whitney began feeling as if she were captive in her own home, constantly under the surveillance of some invisible presence.

"I remember when the house used to be cozy and friendly, but then I felt uncomfortable and on edge in the house—as if someone had taken over my home and I was just an unwelcomed guest visiting," Whitney recalled. "After I knew I wasn't alone, I figured I would try to communicate with the spirit to see what it wanted, and maybe then it would leave. Or so I hoped."

Whitney was an avid viewer of paranormal shows and, after experiencing a few odd events, Whitney decided that she would try to record EVPs with her analog voice recorder, as she had seen on television. She wanted to speak with the presence in her home and perhaps bring resolution to the situation. During their recording sessions they captured several spirit voices. In one of the audio recordings, Whitney asked the spirit, "Can you tell us who you are?" The entity immediately responded in a harsh, dry voice: "No!"

This particular EVP concerned me because most spirits have no qualms about sharing their personal information. They usually are happy to finally communicate with someone who is willing and able to listen to them. Demons, on the other hand, despise giving their names because it enables a person to gain power or control over the demon. Demons will avoid revealing their name at all costs.

Later, on the same audio recording, Whitney and David comment on a strange thump sound they heard:

David: "Did you hear that?"
Whitney: "No ..."
David: "Sounded like somebody knocking at the door!"

Five distinct knocks are heard in the background.
Demon: "Come in!"
The sound of a door opening is heard.

At the time of recording, Whitney and David had only heard the first initial thump on the door. They did not hear the second round of knocking or the door opening. What was equally disturbing was that the knocking sound was identical to when someone knocks five times and someone else knocks back twice in response—the "shave and a haircut, two bits" rhythm. It was darkly playful.

The activity became more severe, and progressed into an aggressive nature after they attempted to interact with the entity by conducting EVP sessions. The more attention they gave the entity, the more disruptive it became. It was growing in strength and force.

One morning, Whitney was taking a bath when she saw several dark shadows standing outside of the shower. The shadows moved in front of the shower curtain, blocking out the light from the bathroom vanity. Whitney instinctively knew these figures were not her son or husband. Panic began to settle in. She called out to her husband, unsure of what to do as she was too frightened to leave the shower. David entered the bathroom and reassured Whitney that nothing was out of place and no intruders were in the bathroom. The shadows were gone.

"See? Look. There is no one in here. You're fine. The heating vents were probably just moving the shower curtain and it looked like someone was in here." David tried calming Whitney but provided her with no relief. Whitney was positive that she saw figures outside the shower. Whitney returned to her routine of getting ready that day. As time passed that afternoon, she began to doubt her own experience and reasoned that she was severely sleep deprived. Whitney was losing rest lately, waking up in the early hours of the morning without an explanation. She assumed it was related to the stress of trying to finish the house and diminishing finances. *Maybe I am losing my mind. I need to get some sleep,* Whitney thought to herself.

Days passed and Whitney found herself performing her daily ritual of getting ready again while David was at work. She headed into the master bedroom to get dressed after her shower, patting her face dry. As she removed her towel to put her clothes on, she heard a distinct wolf-whistle—as if someone were being sexually suggestive towards her. Whitney got the chills, and the feeling of being violated engulfed her. She was home alone and the whistling came from directly behind her in the bedroom. Afraid of possibly seeing the ethereal intruder, Whitney quickly dressed herself and ran downstairs, pretending not to hear the perverse whistle. The entity was making its presence known more frequently and in more direct ways, which unsettled Whitney.

Soon, Whitney began awakening at exactly 3:00 a.m. every morning. She could feel an evil presence in the bedroom with her. Dark shadows would commonly appear next to the television in the master bedroom. David would always be fast asleep during these encounters. Whitney could not wake him up some nights and I wondered if David was experiencing the same "psychic sleep" that my ex-boyfriend Jack had experienced. Whitney would shake and pinch David, trying to rouse him from his sleep, but he would remain in a deep slumber. Whitney would shut her eyes tightly, hoping that the shadows would disappear once she opened her eyes again. Instead, the shadows would be located in different parts of the bedroom, as if they teleported, further terrifying Whitney. Trying to ignore the spirits she rolled over and tucked her head into David's shoulder and tried falling back asleep. It was becoming a regular occurrence.

One evening, Whitney had forgotten to turn off the T.V. before drifting off to sleep. When 3:00 a.m. rolled around, Whitney found herself awake again. She rubbed her eyes trying to make out the television and realized there was something dark blocking the screen. As she cleared her eyes and strained to make sense of what she was seeing, she saw a figure directly in front of the television. The black silhouette growled. She stared in horror and watched as the entity took its long, slender hand and dragged its fingers across the screen. Whitney shrieked and ran downstairs, leaving David still sleeping in the bed. David never woke up. She spent the night downstairs on the couch and regretfully told David the story in the morning.

"Its fingers were long and narrow, almost skeletal," Whitney explained while rubbing her arms from goose bumps. Her abhorrence and fear of the entity was obvious. During our investigative walk-through of the house, we were able to see the finger marks left on the dusty television screen. Granted, anyone could create such a mark on the T.V. with a small object like a pointed ear swab. Whitney assured us she had genuinely experienced the entity's harassment.

There was no benefit or reward in lying to us about some fabricated haunting—she wasn't getting paid for her story, it wasn't going to be publicized, and her only motive was to have us perform a private house blessing. Whitney was terrified in her own home and began altering her routine around the entity. Slowly it was gaining control of her life. It was then that David finally considered Whitney's suggestion to look for outside help.

At last, Whitney began searching online to find someone who could help with their haunting. She wasn't sure where to even begin her search. Finally, after spending some time on the internet, she came across the M.P.R.A. site and decided to contact me.

While Whitney was writing her first message to me, she heard growling by the stairs and then her computer started to behave strangely. "It kept shutting itself off, the internet wouldn't work and finally the keyboard was not typing correctly!" Whitney had to rewrite her e-mail nearly five times until it was successfully sent to me. "I think something was trying to stop me from contacting you guys!" Whitney was adamant and I agreed with her. I had numerous clients mention how electronics and communications failed when they tried to contact me for help with their hauntings.

Hearing Whitney talk, I was unsure if we were dealing with one demonic presence or several. Based on the multiple shadow figures Whitney was seeing, I assumed it was an "infestation"—that several demonic entities were actually present within the home.

Carl and Mike suggested that we listen to the remaining audio recordings to see if we could verify that there were multiple entities. Carl asked Whitney if she could retrieve the additional tapes that she recorded. She soon returned with an audiotape and a video recording.

"We recorded a video in the storage room next to our master bedroom. You can actually see a shadow figure move!" Whitney exclaimed. I had forgotten that she mentioned the videotapes in her original message and this renewed my interest in the footage she captured. We hooked up the camera to the television and began playing back the film.

For nearly half an hour the camera sat still, when suddenly the camera shifted. Whitney and David had positioned the camera to face a mirror in the corner of the room. The room was extremely dark and we strained our eyes to make out the camera's footage. Eventually, a pitch-black figure moved in front of the camera and then disappeared out of the camera's frame. Carl, Mike, and I all sat up straight in excitement and awe. Not only had the family captured legitimate EVPs, but they also had credible footage of their haunting.

Carl sat on the couch listening intently to the additional audio recordings that Whitney and David had documented. "You have to hear this!" Carl announced. I grabbed the headphones and Carl began playing back the segment. To my disbelief, I heard a distinct pig-grunting sound that I had only read about in demonology books. I never understood how or why demons made these audible sounds, but the EVP confirmed we were not dealing with a human spirit. With her permission, I used my digital voice recorder to record the playback of Whitney's EVPs. I wanted to take a copy of the recordings home and review the audio in further detail.

As Whitney and David shared their stories with us in the living room, I had been quietly watching and observing their son Stephen. Stephen was nearly twenty-nine years old by my guess and didn't appear to be very happy. Based on his personal energy and expressions, I sensed that he might be unsure of where he stood in this world.

Stephen was distant and uninterested in the cleansing and our intentions to help his mother, as if his mother's terrors weren't a concern of his. "It doesn't ever bother me," Stephen explained in a complacent manner when I asked him if he would like to have the entity removed from the home. Perhaps he enjoyed seeing his mother being tormented, or maybe he felt a connection with the entity and it was now manipulating him. I wasn't sure. Regardless, it seemed as though he didn't truly want the entity to leave. I was apprehensive of his objectives. *Why wouldn't you want something dark to leave your house and to stop tormenting your family?*

Carl, Mike, and I all perceived a certain darkness that surrounded Stephen and yet none of us could pinpoint exactly what it was. I felt that Stephen might be withholding information from us when discussing the entity in their home, as if he were avoiding the truth. Sometimes it felt as if he were trying to challenge the belief that this entity was negative. I was here to help the family, and I could not force Stephen to cooperate.

But I also could not guarantee a successful cleansing with Stephen's stance and opposing feelings about the entity.

I had asked Whitney over the phone if she and her family believed in a Higher Power and she stated, "Yes we do." I then heard her mumble something about Stephen "complying" when it came to saying a group prayer at the end of the cleansing. I found the statement to be odd and later realized what she was referring to. During our phone call, Whitney had given me the impression that Stephen wasn't religious but he was just spiritual—which was completely fine with me. However, during our visit I was shocked to discover that Stephen was not spiritual, nor did he believe in a Higher Power at all. Stephen was a recent atheist and found it very difficult to agree to recite a nondenominational prayer at the end of the blessing. The group prayer at the end of a cleansing asks a Higher Power to remove any evil inside the home. I had hoped that Stephen would consider participating in the prayer for the sake of his mother's well-being. I specifically brought and used that prayer because almost anyone from any belief can use it. I respect athiests but was unsure how to handle the situation. Stephen clearly believed in some sort of spiritual realm, having experienced the entity and knew of the harm it was doing to his mother, and yet he didn't seem to want it to leave.

I excused myself outside, saying that I had forgotten some supplies in the car, and had Mike and Carl come with me. We all agreed that we were not sure the cleansing would work if Stephen wasn't in agreement with his parents and did not believe in a divine force, but we decided we would try our best to help the family. While we were outside, our digital voice recorder was unknowingly still recording inside the home. I later heard Stephen's protest after reviewing the voice recorder at home. After Whitney begged him to "just go along with it and say the prayer," Stephen replied: "I think it is bullshit that I have to pray and pretend in some God! I do not want to fucking do it!"

As much as Whitney wanted to believe that Stephen was spiritual and that he would not affect the house blessing results, these things cannot be forced.

Carl, Mike, and I returned back inside after gathering our thoughts and method for approaching this delicate case. We were ready to begin the house cleansing, but we had a few remaining questions. I would try to connect with Stephen to see if we were able to pinpoint what his exact beliefs were, and thus we could customize the blessing so we were not offensive or imposing.

"Stephen, do you believe in a positive energy or a higher being that exists in this world?" I asked him, trying to be gentle about such a delicate subject.

"I believe in energy, but I don't think it's good or evil. I think it is all the same." This stumped me and I tried altering the prayer so that Stephen could participate in it without feeling forced or coerced into a foreign religion. I feel it is very important to be respectful of every client's beliefs and to never impart my beliefs on him or her. Upon further review, Stephen relayed that he used to believe in God but no longer did. "Too many bad things happen in life for there to be a real god." This saddened me, because I never want someone to feel they are alone in life or that Great Spirit has forgotten them.

It's very common to see clients turn away from God because they believe that He is at fault for someone's death, illness, or a tragic event. People become confused and assume that God was the one that allowed something terrible to happen. I believe that we actually choose to experience certain events and lessons in our life before being born, some of which are very painful, to further develop our "soul." Great Spirit always gives us a choice—not that we will consciously remember these choices. No one should blame God for their losses or painful experiences, as there is always a greater reason as to why things happen here on Earth, even though we may not understand at that time. There is always a reason, there is always a lesson, and we are constantly learning.

"You are very right, there are a lot of dark and ugly things that happen in this world, much of which is caused by us humans. Sometimes it becomes overwhelming, but it's important to keep your head and heart above it all. As long as you have something to believe in that motivates and inspires you, you can make it through." I made a truce with Stephen and left it at that. I turned my attention back to the entire family.

"Well, it does sound like you have a demon. You have heard scratching, two-footed steps with claws, growling, black figures, perverse whistling, and so on. Is there anything else that you have experienced that we haven't covered?" I asked. Whitney sat in contemplation for a while and then her eyes widened.

"I forgot this! One day I was coming upstairs with the clean laundry and set the clothes on the bed to fold. As I stood there folding the clothes, I began hearing a weird sound in that storage room next to our bedroom." The storage room reminded me of an attic area but was on the same level as their bedroom. It led directly to the roof of the home. There were no signs of pests in the room, but lots of noises originated from there, according to the family. "I moved closer to the storage room door and stopped, trying to hear the sound better. I didn't hear anything for a while until I leaned my head against the door. Suddenly I heard this heavy panting and patting sounds. Then I heard grunting sounds! God, this gives me the creeps! It—it sounded like someone was masturbating in the storage room! I remember I gasped out loud in shock but the noise kept getting louder. Like it enjoyed freaking me out!"

David rubbed Whitney's shoulder to try to comfort her as she struggled to share the story. It was obvious that Whitney was severely disturbed. "I couldn't finish putting away the laundry until David came home." Whitney's life was being controlled by the entity.

Stephen seemed to lack any reaction or feelings of sympathy while sitting there listening to his mother share her experiences. Perhaps I did not understand their relationship, but Stephen was behaving unconcerned, which unsettled me greatly.

"Another thing we experienced," David said as he looked over at Whitney, "sometimes we would feel a fist punching us through the bed mattress or underneath the couch. I had missed having Whitney sleep in bed next to me, so I would try and cuddle her on the couch. Whenever I would try to snuggle up with her, something would pound underneath the cushions! And I mean, there was literally a fist punching the bottom of the couch! How do you explain that?" David was perplexed.

I tried reassuring them that they weren't insane and their accounts were valid. I told them of a famous demonic case in which the family wasn't permitted much sleep because they felt a fist punching underneath their bed. I reasoned that if a demon can keep a couple from sleeping or bonding with each other, all the better. The client becomes emotionally and physically exhausted, and the demon hopes that you will give in to their harassment. I then asked David and Whitney to explain their health, finances, and any experiences with the occult.

"Well, after we tore into the fireplace, both Whitney and I started having trouble at our workplaces. In the midst of all these weird experiences, she and I *both* lost our jobs. It was devastating." The entity had succeeded in oppressing the family in various ways. "We started having issues with severe depression after that. I couldn't find work and Whitney wanted to keep working on the house, but we just did not have the money to do it. We're still struggling."

As we continued our discussion with the family, David addressed the fact that his best friend Matt used to read the "black bible," or a satanic bible. Matt frequently visited the home and grew up with David. "He was into some darker shit. I remember when he started getting into that stuff, I didn't really know what to say. I was hoping it was just fictional and had no power."

David continued describing his relationship with Matt. Although he never said this directly, it was implied to us that David involved himself in Matt's dark practices. David then revealed a crucial piece of information to the case. "The shadows I've seen have been following me for twenty-five to thirty years now." He had been experiencing these dark entities most of his life and the timing seemed to correlate with Matt's dabbling in Satanism. *Was this whole haunting a result of David's past with Matt and the dark arts?* I was unsure I would be able to find an answer, but it seemed that the house blessing had quite a dirty laundry list to clean.

Some individuals who involve themselves in satanic rituals assume that over the years the consequences or "side effects" of such practices subside, or magically go away. Although I have seen individuals leave the dark arts and turn themselves towards good, sometimes it is critical to verbally denounce your involvement with evil and to formally accept Spirit back into your life. God is always waiting and forgiving, but there seems to be a needed "announcement" or verbal declaration that you have changed your ways for it to fully work.

Stephen's lack of faith and desire to help, combined with David's possible indirect involvement with evil proved to be a double whammy, but we informed the family that we would do our best to remove the entities despite these circumstances. They didn't have anything to lose and we wanted to help the family with our greatest efforts.

Finally, we were all on the same page and came to an agreement that a house blessing should still be performed. I began preparing my house blessing items and I could tell that Stephen grew more nervous.

Many of the rooms in the house were filled with debris and renovation materials, making it difficult for us to access the entirety of each room. Climbing over piles and trash, we pressed forward with the blessing. Soon the house was saturated in the white sage aroma and I felt that whatever entity resided in the home was in hiding. I was expecting a fierce confrontation from the demon but was surprised when we experienced no intimidation or antics. The house was very quiet, something I was not used to.

As we entered the upstairs storage room and attic, I made sure to waft the smoke into the rafters for several minutes—just to be thorough. Perhaps the demon was hiding in the attic above the master bedroom, but I had no means of accessing that area.

Carl, Mike, and I all repeated our prayers and commands out loud, demanding that the entities leave the home. I was accustomed to feeling a dramatic change in the home once the entity left. *Maybe it's already gone …* I thought to myself, but I was always skeptical and held my breath. The house felt lighter, happier, and brighter, but I didn't feel a remarkable release from the demon leaving. Like Whitney, I had also been losing a lot of sleep over the case prior to our visit, and perhaps my senses were dulled down from the lack of rest. Maybe I could not sense it leaving; I was burned out. I asked

Carl and Mike what they thought and they said they felt pretty good about the cleansing, but were also undecided.

After finishing with the olive oil and salt, I then began making my rounds through the house while using holy water. Perhaps I have obsessive-compulsive disorder, but I always have the need to be thorough.

Carl and Mike continued their path through the house, praying out loud and wafting the dried sweet grass smoke into the air. Sweet grass is a wonderful herb to promote happiness and to bring positive energy into a home. I hoped this was the final step needed to remove the entity.

Stephen left the house to have a cigarette outside and the door slammed behind him. It bothered me that we didn't have his full participation. It felt as if he were thinking, *Well, let the crazies do their thing and let's just get this over with. This is just really stupid.* I wish I had been permitted to have a heart-to-heart talk with Stephen that day. However, he wasn't open to it and I could not force light and love into his life unless he was inviting and accepting. I tried to concentrate on finishing the blessing as I completed the master bedroom. Minutes passed and finally I felt inner quiet and solitude. I prayed that the entities were gone.

We announced that we had finished doing the blessing and could now close with the prayer. I asked if we could all sit together in the living room, indicating to Whitney and David to grab their paper copy of the prayer. We had to wait for Stephen to return from his cigarette break, and I am sure he was reluctant about even coming back into the house. Eventually, he situated himself on the recliner and awaited our initiation. As usual, I had the clients lead us in the prayer and we all repeated after Whitney. Throughout the prayer, Stephen seemed distracted and would look about the room as if he were daydreaming and preoccupied with thoughts like *I need to get my oil changed. Next week I should probably call the dentist.* Then again, I might have been reading into Stephen's expression too much, but I could only wonder what was going on inside his head. Maybe I didn't want to know.

I remember praying to myself that day. *"God, please help Stephen remember that you are real. Come into his life and show him. Give him a sign that he cannot dismiss. Remove any darkness, depression, or evil from his life and help him. Heal him."* I had hoped that something in Stephen's life would turn around and maybe he would remember the good in this world, and that someone was indeed watching over him. I reminded myself that not everyone could be helped and I focused on the present moment. The house's energy was definitely different and I felt much more peaceful.

"Can you guys feel it too? The house is lighter!" Whitney asked us with excitement.

I will never get tired of the sensation after a house blessing, no matter how many I perform. It is a feeling of light, love, happiness, peace, relaxation (yet energizing), and all the good feelings wrapped into a little bundle. It feels like the presence of God, which I can only describe as pure beauty and love.

David and Whitney continued commenting on how the impression of the house had changed. Carl, Mike, and I were delighted to help another family.

"I cannot wait to get a good night's sleep! And in the same bed as David!" Whitney now reminded me of a giddy schoolgirl and I couldn't help but smile. Whitney achieved independence again. She could now shower alone, sleep in the same bed as David, be in the house by herself, and go back to her normal life.

I was pleased to receive a testimonial e-mail from Whitney the next day:

"I want to thank the Michigan P.R.A. for helping us so quickly. They are a very professional group and did a wonderful job of getting rid of the demon in our house. The blessing of the house was a blessing."

I continued checking in with Whitney to see how her house was doing and if anything had happened. The night after the blessing, Whitney woke up around 3:00 a.m. again. She looked around the room, expecting her usual visitors, but was pleasantly surprised to find that she and David were finally alone. Whitney's internal clock would need to readjust itself and not wake her up at 3:00 a.m. anymore, but that was something she could get used to. Whitney reassured us that the haunting was finally gone and it was a relief.

I had left Whitney some white sage, salt, and instructions to use as protection in case anything happened in the future. She slept soundly with the items next to the bed on her nightstand.

Over half a year passed, and I received a disheartening e-mail from Whitney on February 27, 2011:

> *"I haven't put the camera up there; I don't know if I want to,*
> *I'm still debating. I put the recorder in the bedroom and*
> *when I left I turned the recorder on. The next morning, I*
> *went up there and it was on, but the recorder only recorded*
> *the last five minutes. You could hear me coming up the steps.*
> *The recorder is a fifteen-hour recorder. Something shut it off*
> *and turned it back on ... Well, IT'S BACK ... It isn't as bad as*
> *it was, though. I have claw marks all over my TV again, and*
> *it's noisy up there, but nothing really tries to scare just me. I*
> *haven't heard any whispers ... just thumps and the marks on*
> *the TV. When I'm up there I get the same creepy feeling."*

I found out that Stephen had moved out for six months and had just returned home. About the same time, Whitney and David had begun to experiment with EVPs again. Following the EVP sessions and attempts at communicating with the spirit world, the dark entity returned to their house. It was an open invitation for the demon to return—likely because they didn't use any protection before conducting spirit communication or because it had attached itself to Stephen and returned home with him.

I realized that without a family's full participation and commitment to keeping the entity away, the haunting could return. I could not prevent them from experimenting with recording EVPs and the paranormal, even if there were consequences. Whitney asked me for directions again on how to perform her own blessing and I gladly gave her some tips and steps to follow.

I informed Whitney that if she wished to continue spirit communication against my recommendations, she should perform some protection prayers to prevent negative entities from indulging. Here's the protection prayer I gave her:

"God, I pray that only positive, white light spirits may communicate with us and prevent any dark or negative spirits from contacting us. Amen."

I have not heard from Whitney since and she never requested another house blessing. I consider that a good sign. I hope their home is finally at peace.

CHAPTER 5

LANSING, MICHIGAN CASE

It had been an extremely busy winter with paranormal cases and I was growing tired of the constant battle against "the dark side"—as if I were in some warped *Star Wars* movie (although, personally, I'm a fan of *Lord of the Rings*). Michigan's winter was slowly beating me down and I found myself overloaded with requests for house blessings, on top of entering my final semester in college.

I could not wait to finally graduate and I could see the light at the end of the tunnel. In an effort to prioritize the most severe cases and my personal life, I found myself handling the request of Kacey and her daughter Shannon. On January 29, 2011, we met at Kacey's home to discuss their haunting and to provide a house blessing.

When we arrived, both Carl and I felt the tension of a recent argument in the home and it was uncomfortable to walk into. Shannon was nineteen years old and had a two-year-old daughter, Holly—both of whom lived in Kacey's home in a small suburb of Lansing. The relationship between Kacey and Shannon was extremely strained and they constantly fought on a daily basis. I admired Kacey's efforts at being a good mother and grandmother. Kacey explained to us that Shannon wasn't required to pay any rent, bills, food expenses, or utilities—she simply lived at her mom's house for free with Holly.

She also mentioned that Shannon frequently criticized Kacey, physically attacked her, and was emotionally abusive. In addition to not having a job, Kacey complained that Shannon would often relax around the house while Kacey took care of Holly and the basic chores. There was definitely a power struggle between Shannon and Kacey, and it was apparent during our visit.

"Just shut the hell up already, Kacey!" Shannon screamed at her mom.

Shannon's disrespect and hatred was unpalatable, but many households across America exist in this state of dismay, especially when a demon is present. All I could see was Kacey's kindness and generosity towards her daughter and granddaughter, but perhaps I wasn't seeing the situation's entirety.

I had suspicion that a darker entity was influencing Shannon's behavior and that she had lost touch with reality. Her angry tirades and physical attacks on her mother and boyfriend led me to believe that the entity was feeding off her energy and manipulating her.

I had to embody a leadership role, calm and assertive, to stop the bickering between Kacey and Shannon. "While Carl and I are here, both of you will take turns speaking. I don't want you interrupting each other, because both of your stories and opinions are important to us and we want to make sure we hear everyone's side." I continued, "Try to be respectful and to not accuse each other, but rather you are working together as a team to get rid of this haunting."

I calmly explained the process and hoped that we would get through the interview smoothly. Most families try to be civil while we are present, but that is not always the case. I deal with severely dysfunctional families and, fortunately, my experience with counseling comes in handy quite often. I try teaching communication techniques, coping mechanisms, and a variety of tools for families to use—I have helped numerous families regain their composure and trust.

"So let's begin!" I cheerfully announced, trying to put everyone at ease. I asked Shannon for a description of some of the most severe experiences she had while present in the house. Shannon raised her eyes towards the ceiling and began pondering her response.

Shannon's first experiences were seeing shadows in the home—similar to full figures, but they were very dark, just like shadows. She had also seen a face in the ceiling of her bedroom and eventually began hearing things. Shannon was able to list off her experiences effortlessly as if she had shared this information with someone before. The house was quite active, and especially rambunctious when Shannon was home.

One day Shannon was getting changed in her room when she heard some noises on Holly's baby monitor. Shannon continued dressing herself and ignored the white-noise sounds until it grew louder. It was difficult to ignore. As she listened more closely she heard a distinct voice come over the receiver and say, "Touch her!" It was a deep, gravelly voice that sounded rough. Shannon, in a moment of panic, ran from her room without the rest of her clothes and began sobbing to Kacey.

"I remember that day very well," Kacey confirmed. "I was hoping that Shannon had just been hearing noises and mistook it as something else. But things continued and the house began to feel different."

Shannon also heard conversations on the baby monitor. When she and her mom tried listening to the discussion, it sounded like two men talking about something in a low tone. Kacey and Shannon sat there listening to the baby monitor and after a few moments, a growling sound began in the room they were standing in. The growling was not on the baby monitor. Shannon said it was like "it" knew they were listening to the conversation. It became angry and came in to the room growling at them. Both Shannon and Kacey agreed it sounded like a dog or some kind of animal.

Shannon shivered with chills when retelling their accounts. I had seen so many clients share similar reactions— these people were truly afraid for their safety on a daily basis and their lives were forever altered. Whether the spirits and entities were removed or not, the experience of a haunting changes people.

As the two women continued sharing their stories I began to mend together facts and incidents that pointed towards the possibility of a demon being present in their home. Growling sounds have always indicated a dark and evil entity in our cases and is a phenomena that people should be cautious of. I have yet to experience a "human haunting" in which the spirit growled.

Whenever Shannon would visit her father's separate house, the entity would follow her to his home. On one occasion both Shannon and her father witnessed what appeared to be a dark, hooded creature floating out of the house. They refused to go inside for several hours and instead they drove around in their car debating what to do next and where to receive help. "How do you get rid of something when you don't even know what it is!" Shannon explained. The entity was tall, extremely dark, had no face and seemed to glide above the ground as it moved. It made Shannon's skin crawl and its presence emanated the feeling of evil.

Black orbs were frequently seen in Kacey's home, and even their family dog took notice. About three weeks prior to our visit, their dog Bonnie tried eating one of the orbs that flew past her face. Everyone who was present saw it. Kacey insisted that there was no possibility those "things" were bugs or just a light reflection.

Orbs are interesting phenomena. Some paranormal researchers believe that the color of "orbs" is indicative of their nature—black or dark orbs consist of negative energy. In my experience, this theory seems to hold true in that many black masses and orbs have been seen with demonic cases.

The light anomalies became more common and Kacey's family could no longer ignore their presence. They tried capturing a photograph of the orb. Instead of an orb appearing in the picture, they discovered that a foreign and "alienlike" silhouette was reflected in the mirror.

I examined the image thoroughly and determined that it was not a double exposure, the image was also in the negative, and it was not the reflection of someone in the room at the time the photograph was taken. At first glance, the picture seemed to be legitimate. Had I more time, I would have loved to take it to a specialist for examination. For now, it was just additional evidence that Kacey's family was experiencing something not of this world.

The sounds of growling pervaded throughout the home for weeks on end and the family even hired a pest control company to inspect their home for any wild animals in the attic. Nothing was found during the pest control's exploration of the home and Kacey and Shannon were left without answers. Nothing seemed to make sense in their home anymore—paranormal incidents were becoming a weekly occurrence and it was taking a toll on the family. As with many cases, they began to doubt their own sanity and started to hate the idea of being in Kacey's house.

One evening Shannon was playing with her daughter Holly when suddenly the child became distracted and gazed up at the stairwell. Holly ran to her mother and cried out in a frightened and trembling voice, "I'm scared!" Shannon tried comforting the girl in her arms and asked what she was afraid of. Holly pointed up the stairs and Shannon was horrified to see blue smoke drifting in the air.

At first Shannon thought her eyes were tired, but confusion quickly followed. A few feet off the top step, a mass of swirling blue "mist" was hovering. Within seconds the cloud evaporated into thin air as if some invisible vacuum had cleared away the image. Shannon hastily grabbed her child and ran outside until Kacey returned home from work. Shannon didn't know how to explain to her mother what she and her child had seen. Again, it was unnatural and the feeling of it was malicious.

Throughout random hours of the day and evening, both women would find themselves running to the kitchen to see if something had caught on fire. Nauseating smells of burning rubber and sulfur were permeating throughout the house without a viable cause. I have yet to explain why demonic cases incorporate such foul smells, other than to offend and confuse the victims into a further state of fear.

In addition to the odors, Shannon began experiencing strange mood swings and bouts of depression. The haunting was escalating.

Shannon recalled an experience in which she became severely depressed for three days. She wasn't upset with Holly or her mom, and it wasn't because of any relationship issues with her boyfriend. Shannon was just extremely sad for three days and she could not figure out why. Even her dreams were macabre and disturbing. She did not want to live anymore and was happy with the idea of being gone from this world. It seemed as though the demonic entity was not only influencing her emotions but also beginning to have an effect on her thought process and decision-making. The demon's ability to manipulate Shannon was becoming stronger.

As Shannon's personal experiences with the haunting became more severe, the fights between her and Kacey intensified. Surprisingly, Kacey did not call the police when Shannon hit and slapped her during their arguments. Kacey felt that whomever she was dealing with was not her daughter, and she did not want to see Shannon go to jail for something she might not be able to control. "She just did not look like herself when she was angry and trying to hurt me! It was not my daughter!" Kacey insisted that she never raised her daughter to hit anyone, and yet Shannon was beating her.

I asked Shannon if she remembered these fights; specifically, hitting her mother and the things she said during the arguments.

"No, not really. I remember getting upset, but after that point everything seems like a blur. I remember feeling rage and hatred and it would be over the dumbest things in hindsight, but I just could not stand to be around my mom." Shannon blatantly stated, "I still can't."

I explained that sometimes I see cases in which an individual is pitted against the person that loves them the most to break down that bond and relationship so that the family further deteriorates. I tried reaching Shannon on a personal level to see if I could still get through to her personal emotions, and not the emotions of a demon. I told Shannon that I couldn't think of someone who loved her more than her own mother.

Shannon seemed uninterested. Either she was putting on a facade of being tough or the demon had really shut off her emotions from the rest of the world and was controlling her greater than I thought.

"And Kacey, you know that your daughter really does love you. Sometimes daughters and sons say terrible things to try to hurt us because they themselves are hurting inside. Even though you two are going through a tough time right now, who else would be here for you? Who else would be as supportive as your own family?"

I continued trying to rationalize with Shannon. "Your friends seem to be too scared to come over and visit anymore, Shannon. But you two have each other and surprisingly that will be the key to getting out of this whole mess in the end. That and asking God to help." Shannon seemed to grow annoyed with my statement and rose from her chair while maintaining eye contact with me. She had a scowl on her face and went to the kitchen. After Shannon left, Carl, Kacey, and I decided to visit the basement to discuss one of the other active rooms. Kacey had been kind enough to begin refinishing a room for Holly—the renovation was also questionable in terms of what instigated the paranormal activity.

In the corner of the basement, Holly's playroom stood, and adjacent from it was a very odd and peculiar room. The door to the strange room was covered with blankets. I asked why it was concealed from view. "Oh, it's because Holly and Shannon were seeing evil faces in the door's window. So we covered it up," Kacey explained. I asked if I could examine the room.

Apparently, the room had previously been an underground garage but was now sealed in. I proceeded into the cement room. The energy of the room was imbalanced and there were no outside windows to lighten up the space. I felt that the demon likely resided in there, especially in such a dark room—demons love darkness and a lack of sunlight, much like cockroaches. I felt the strong presence, to a great extent the same as I did when walking into the home; however, it seemed more concentrated in this space.

I agreed to take "extra special time" in that room during the blessing, a term I jokingly used when describing the dungeon-of-hell vibe I often felt in areas like this. Think of a cozy and quaint den that a bear hibernates in during the winter—except the bear is demonic and the den is really an ice-cold abyss that sucks the life and happiness out of its surroundings. The space desperately needed attention!

I have always hated the anticipation and build-up of energy right before a blessing. It is similar to having an out of control child running rampant around the house waiting for me to enforce discipline. The demon was constantly moving around the house and sometimes I fantasized about having one of those child harnesses on the demon so it would just sit still during my assessment. But alas, it is never that easy to control an unseen force, let alone one that should not be taken lightly. These forces are capable of harming people, ending the life of someone, and greatly influencing others.

I explored for more details and asked Kacey what kind of faces they were seeing.

"This is what really scared me when Shannon told me. Shannon was playing down here with Holly one time and kept getting distracted. She kept feeling like something was terribly wrong but had no idea why. Almost as if someone was about to die and she was picking up on it with her sixth sense, I guess? Finally, she looked up and saw this creature's face in the window to the garage room. She described it as having a really long giraffe's neck but the face was ancient and reptilian looking. Almost a cross between a snake, alligator, and gecko's face. She said that it had water pouring out of its mouth. I don't know. I just hate that room with a passion. I never go in there, which is why it is completely empty. I won't even use it for storage."

Everyone seemed to be severely uncomfortable with the room and I was now certain that the demon truly did reside there. Although we had found the most concentrated room, I still wanted to find out why the entity had come into their lives. We went back upstairs to escape the black void leaking from the garage room and met in the living room. The basement's cold grasp was hard to shake off as we ascended the stairs. The negative energy emanating from it felt like a very icy, damp fog that clung to bones and flesh.

I questioned whether or not Kacey was experiencing anything odd at her place of work or if any strange activity occurred. I wanted to see to what extent the haunting was affecting Kacey. In some difficult hauntings, the activity has occasionally taken place at the victim's place of employment.

"Well that is something I wanted to talk with you about," Kacey paused and stared at her feet beneath her clasped hands. "I would feel terrible if this was the reason why ... but I work at a cemetery. You don't think it could be the reason why things are so strange here, do you?" Kacey tried containing her tears. Her sense of guilt was saddening. *How horrible it would be to feel responsible for a terrifying haunting that is scaring your daughter and granddaughter.*

"Kacey, no matter what job you have, no matter where you live, you are never solely responsible for a haunting." I raised my eyebrows and lowered my head to meet her eyes. "Okay?" I explained that spirits and demons alike both have a mind of their own and if they decide to haunt a location that is their decision; it was not her decision or her responsibility.

Spirits are everywhere, even at the grocery store or car wash. If they follow someone, that is something the spirit chose, unless that individual invited them. I told Kacey that I would like to teach her some techniques on how to protect herself more and how to keep out the bad things.

Kacey nodded her head quietly and I hoped to calm her feelings of remorse and shame. It was possible that the entity followed Kacey home from work, but it seemed as though Shannon was feeding the entity and giving it a permanent reason to stay with the family. I had experienced demons at cemeteries before, although I did not realize it at the time.

I began sharing my story with Kacey. One evening when I was in high school, my mother, boyfriend, and I decided that we wanted to visit a notorious cemetery nearby in Michigan in hopes of capturing an EVP. Concerned for the three of us and the possibility of getting arrested, my father insisted that he chaperone us to the graveyard and keep an eye out for us. My dad is a logical man. He is a retired engineer and inventor, has over sixteen international patents, and is a member of MENSA. At that time he was not entertaining the idea of ghosts and ghouls. But that would soon change.

In the courageous minivan we made our way to the cemetery at around ten o'clock in the evening. My mother, hoping she could outsmart the possible dark entities there, placed the voice recorder on the tombstone of a reverend—praying his holiness would protect our asinine efforts. Boy, were we wrong! We left the recorder there for about two hours and returned around midnight after having coffee and some dessert. When we revisited that night, the entire feeling of the cemetery had changed and all of us had felt the transformation.

My mom was incredibly nervous and dropped her purse; she scurried to gather the discarded items back into her bag before jumping into the car. We ran and grabbed the recorder and took off in the van. *So brave.*

At around three in the morning, I woke up to the loud sound of something crashing on the floor. I went upstairs to investigate but did not find anything out of place or broken. I begrudgingly went back to sleep. Later that morning, over the conversation of breakfast, I asked if anyone else had heard that sound. My father paused from eating his pancake and put down his fork. "Oh my god, I completely forgot about that!" My mom chimed in and also declared that she had forgotten. Apparently, while my parents were sleeping, my dad awoke to his sleep apnea machine being thrown across the room. The machine weighed a considerable amount and was not within arms-reach of the bed. The device was thrown several feet across the room and it abruptly awoke my dad.

My mother said she just lay there with her eyes shut and kept praying. "I apologized to the spirit and promised that I would never return to that cemetery if it would just leave and go in peace!"

My father also found the event to be unsettling, especially since he was the one targeted in the attack and had forgotten to grab his crucifix necklace before driving us to the cemetery. I, of course, returned to the cemetery in the future to show others, but my mother kept her promise and none of us were bothered again.

I did, however, encounter the same angry presence in that graveyard and, to this day, I believe it was evil in nature. Nearly eight years later my father now questions the experience and his logical, engineer mind has determined that the event is explainable. However, I distinctly remember his reaction the morning after the event—it was genuine.

Sometimes things follow people from cemeteries. As a lesson learned, I always advise people to protect themselves with prayers and the white light before and after dealing with compromising locations such as graveyards.

"So it is possible that it did follow you, Kacey, but I think it stayed because it felt it could influence Shannon." As if we had summoned her, Shannon returned from her absence and joined us back in the living room.

I announced to both Shannon and Kacey that it sounded like the family was dealing with an inhuman entity, after hearing all of their accounts and personal experiences.

"So you are saying that it *is* a demon?" Shannon inquired with a sarcastic tone.

I confirmed with a solemn "yes." The hooded figure she had been seeing, the reptilian face in the basement, the growling sounds, the inappropriate "touch her" statement on the baby monitor ... all of these seemed to point towards a demonic presence. I proceeded to ask Shannon if she had heard any other voices, such as her child's or mother's voice when they were not home. Shannon paused in response to my question and then her eyes grew wider, her sarcasm gone.

"Actually, I do remember something like that." Shannon's voice had changed to a more humble tone. "Kacey had left to go grocery shopping while I was home with Holly one evening. While I was in the kitchen preparing some food for Holly, I heard my mother calling me. I assumed that she had a quick visit to the grocery store and perhaps forgot her wallet and that was the reason she came home so early. I yelled back to her and told her that I was in the kitchen, and asked her what she wanted. She did not respond, so I went into the living room to ask her again what she wanted. No one was home. I went through the entire house and couldn't find her anywhere. But it *was* my mom's voice!"

I continued taking notes as Shannon finished her story. I wanted to know if Kacey had personally encountered any physical attacks—a hallmark of how severe the haunting had become. I asked her if she had any experiences with the entity touching her. I listed clawing, scratches, poking, shoving, and slapping as examples. Kacey nodded her head and hesitantly began reciting her memories.

"Last summer I was taking a nap with Holly while Shannon spent some time with her boyfriend. We were just sleeping on the couch together, all cuddled up. I remember waking up suddenly after I felt a distinct fist or hand punch through the bottom side of the cushion!"

"Oh my God!" Shannon blurted out. "I didn't know you had the same thing happen to you! I have had a fist punch me from *underneath* my bed's mattress!" There seemed to be a connection or trust building between Shannon and Kacey after they shared their similar stories. They had obviously never truly talked about the haunting together and never gave each other the chance to confide in one another.

"It's terrifying," Kacey stated while looking over at Shannon. "It only happened to me that one time … but I don't think I could continue living here if it happened again."

I reassured them both that I came to help Kacey and her family so they didn't have to keep experiencing these things. It is just not healthy living in fear and stress all the time. I didn't want Shannon's child Holly to grow up in a home with such a dark entity and environment. She would start to have memories soon and I wanted those memories to be good ones.

I decided that we should proceed with the blessing after figuring out the religious views of both Kacey and Shannon.

"I do believe in God. I am not religious in that I don't go to church, but I am a firm believer that there is a God. I know Shannon believes in God, but not so much lately." Kacey nodded towards Shannon in hopes that she would explain her views to us as well.

"I believe in God, it's just that … I don't ever seem to get a response when I pray and there are just so many bad things going on that sometimes I feel like He isn't listening." Shannon was resigned. "Like when that paranormal group came over here, everything got really active and I kept praying for God to make it stop, but it only got worse!"

I interrupted Shannon briefly to clarify her statement about a previous paranormal group and the increase of activity—it was an important piece of information.

It completely slipped Kacey's mind, but she went on to explain, "Yes. We had a paranormal group from outside the Lansing area come to do an investigation one evening. Does that cause a problem for the blessing today?"

I explained that it was not a problem at all, but I was curious to find out if they had captured any evidence, had personal experiences, or tried to bless the home. Sometimes paranormal groups will try to bless a home and it doesn't work, so then the activity flares up—along the lines of what Shannon was suggesting.

Shannon explained that the paranormal group got some weird or "abnormal" EMF (electromagnetic field) readings off her bedroom mirror. "We moved the mirror and couldn't find any electrical lines or a reason for why the mirror was giving a high reading." Shannon partly smiled—proud of her recently learned knowledge on paranormal devices and practices. "There were about five of them, and they all started freaking out when their batteries died. They said that the spirit was draining the battery."

Kacey stated that she had seen their own batteries and light bulbs go dead pretty quickly in the house, so she was not too surprised when the investigators said their batteries were dying. She lifted the television remote, suggesting that she had to replace batteries too frequently and it was a source of much frustration for her.

"But they did kind of do a blessing, I think?" Shannon acknowledged. "I remember they brought a Bible and were walking around the house reciting prayers and stuff after they did the investigation that night."

I inquired if the blessing was performed the same evening after the investigation. Shannon nodded and I jotted down the details on my cluttered notepad. I always preferred to bless homes during the daytime, but I understood the group's desire to remove the entity after dealing with it during the investigation.

I asked Shannon and Kacey to sit and pray out loud together when we began the blessing—asking God to come into their home and lives and to remove any evil or dark entities. I reminded them to try to focus as much as they could while we performed the ceremony and if anything happened to keep praying and ignore the activity. Kacey and Shannon nodded, realizing that the final moments of the haunting had finally arrived and perhaps they shared an uncertainty in regards to the long-term results. After having a blessing done previously, some clients begin to doubt the effectiveness of praying and the ceremonies. I began unpacking my blessing supplies, including a charcoal disc that had to be lit.

When I went into the kitchen I found a gas stove with the igniter burnt out. I've always had visions of blowing up the kitchen accidently with gas stoves, despite my love for them in my previous culinary classes. It seems like action movies frequently use the gas line in the kitchen to demolish the place. I had *no* desire to do such a thing. My irrational fears were quickly extinguished when Carl bustled into the kitchen and started up the gas flames. I was relieved.

Holding the charcoal disc over the flame, I got the abalone shell ready. I remember sensing the presence behind me as I was breaking up the white sage smudge stick into small pieces.

As we worked, Carl and I joked amongst ourselves. "Do you feel that?" I asked. "Uncle Ted is here ..." I referred to the demon as if it were some obnoxious relative.

"Yep," Carl replied. "Didn't you know there was a family cookout today?" I always appreciated keeping calm and a sense of humor even when being intimidated by an evil entity.

"Well, I brought a special dish to pass for the cookout, my smoked white sage—Uncle Ted's favorite!" I chuckled and then headed into the living room with Carl.

Once the blessing began I always presented a "game face" attitude and although I was assertive and stern with spirits and entities during a blessing, I was always warm and friendly with the family to comfort them. I think many clients expect a dramatic and theatrical event to unfold during a blessing, similar to an exorcism out of a blockbuster feature. However, my cleansings are quite relaxing and healing for the families.

Instead of the house bursting into demonic flames while I splash the rooms with holy water, the house slowly begins to calm as the white sage smoke gently lulls everyone into a calmer state. It's similar to group meditation or yoga in the morning—with a side of uncertainty—but almost everyone feels at peace.

I heard Shannon and Kacey quietly reciting prayers in the living room and I encouraged them to be as loud as they wanted and to command the demon out with conviction and authority. This was *their* home, not the demon's, and it no longer had any right to be there. The women needed to finally feel in control and to sense that they, too, had a significant role in casting out the entity. I am not some special, holy person. I am just a normal being who wants to help others finally escape the abuse and oppression caused by a demon.

"Are you sure?" Kacey asked with an uncertain tone.

"Yes. Feel free to be as loud as you want. The demon needs to hear you, and to realize that you are *not* going to be bullied anymore. You are taking your life back and you are reclaiming your home. This is when your anger and frustration with the haunting can be proactive and help motivate you."

Kacey began to holler into the spaces throughout her home. "In the name of God...you need to leave *now*, demon! This is *my* home! Not yours! This is my family! Not yours! And this is *my* life! Get out now!"

I was a bit surprised with how much confidence and gusto Kacey performed. It's fun and touching to see some people finally let loose and to climb out from underneath the thumb and oppression of evil. It's like a revelation for them, and I can see the light coming back into their hearts and minds. *I can defend myself...I can help make this entity leave*, they suddenly realize. It is truly liberating.

Even though both women were shouting their prayers and commands, little Holly laid calmly in her mother's lap dosing off to sleep. She was protected. As Kacey and Shannon continued their effort in the battle, Carl and I headed down into the basement to confront the entity head-on.

Although most basements are cooler than the main floor level, I could feel a severe and dramatic drop in temperature as we descended the stairs. The atmosphere had become damp and clammy. The cold clung to the hairs on my arms and I felt weighed down by the heaviness in the air. It reminded me of a time when I fell into extremely cold water and my lungs had a hard time opening for air. I wanted to breathe but it was staggered and I struggled for oxygen.

"Wow..." I muttered to Carl. Carl was silent and I assumed he was experiencing the same intense sensations as I was. I sometimes pictured a demon crouching in the corner of the room, beckoning me with a crooked finger *"come closer..."*

Demons seem to enjoy luring me into their "domain." Demons always seem to have an animalistic quality about them. There is nothing human about them and, aside from their intelligence, they are as foreign as a wild animal pretending to be a human. Although they appear to have "emotions and thoughts" they could care less for human life and obtain all the foulest characteristics you could imagine: jealousy, rage, hatred, gluttony, sexual perversion, violence... the list could go on. The majority of people would never harm an animal and would be nauseated at the thought of taking an innocent puppy's life. Not a demon. They simply do not have any remorse, guilt, or sorrow. It is like an empty, vacant sociopath that would stare you in the eyes and tell you that *it* enjoyed disemboweling your favorite pet.

I have a healthy hatred for demons. But I also, ironically, feel sorry for them because they live such a pointless, miserable existence and are so far from the light of God that the darkness must be all-consuming and dreadful.

When I reached the bottom of the stairs in the basement, we decided to remove the blankets and sheets that were blocking the door's window into the garage room. As the fabric fell to the floor in a pile I saw into the dark and seemingly empty room. However, it was far from empty. I felt the distinct sensation of having stared the entity directly in the eyes, although no visible evidence was there. It felt like I had made eye contact with the serial killer I was about to go to trial against in court. It was literally a face-off.

Carl distracted me as he began anointing the walls in the corner by Holly's playroom with olive oil and his blessed cloth.

I headed towards Carl. As I moved away from the garage room I saw a dark shadow dart past the door. The demon was making a break for it and was trying to find refuge in another area.

"In the name of God, any dark, evil, and unclean spirits must leave this home at once! You have no right to be here. May the light of God shine down upon you and scatter you from this home! By the power of God I command you to leave!" I wafted the heavy plumes of smoke into every corner and felt the smoke sterilizing the darkness and negativity. It almost had a sanitizing effect. "You may not scare or harm this family. You are not allowed to bully them or to subdue them with fear. This is a house of God and you cannot exist amongst the light of God. Where God is present, you shall perish! Leave now!"

As I continued my efforts in the basement, Shannon broke away from her prayers upstairs and kept saying, "Oh God!" I called up to her and asked if she was okay.

"I just keep seeing that screaming face in my mind's eye. It is the same face I saw on my bedroom's ceiling!" Shannon was close to tears.

"Shannon, you have to stay strong!" I yelled to her. "The demon is trying to put up a final fight and you have to be strong. Since it is most attached to you, it will try to intimidate you. Do not feel fear. You will only feed it further. I want you to imagine a bright, white light enveloping you and your entire body. It is the presence of God. Pray that God protects you and helps you through this."

Shannon grew silent and I knew she was battling with the demon inside her mind. It's hard to envision the light of God when being swallowed by darkness. I had finished my rounds with the white sage in the basement, but still needed to bless the garage room. I pulled open the heavy door, which required more effort than I expected. A wave of ice-cold air hit me and traveled through my core. As I entered the room, a stale and terrible smell permeated the air. The room felt heavier than when we examined it during the walkthrough. It seemed as though I were attempting to walk through a dense fog.

"Here we go." Carl valiantly pressed forward and joined me in the room. "It smells terrible in here!"

I agreed and began blowing on to the white sage bundle, trying to encourage more smoke to rise. Amazingly, the smoke began to billow out of the shell and towards the floor, as if I were handling dry ice. Last I knew, heat and smoke were supposed to rise, not sink. "This is really strange. I have never seen that before."

Carl looked to see what I was referring to and I saw his expression change to confusion as he watched the smoke fall towards the floor. "Just keep going and let's clear out this room."

Finally, I ignored the strange behavior of the smoke and headed into each corner. Even wafting the smoke with the feather wand felt heavier than normal. *Then again, what was normal?* During moments like this I nearly accepted any strange phenomena as normal and nothing to fret about—it was how I coped with the oddities I came across in the paranormal world. Sasquatch could have strolled into the room with an evening suit on and I probably would try to stay calm and continue on with the blessing. I had to stay focused.

Carl went through each area with the olive oil and his blessed cloth and finished the blessing in the room. It was a relief to feel the room lighten and to actually breathe comfortable air. I no longer felt like I was stuck in some meat locker, but rather, I was in a normal basement. Although I do not like entertaining investigations with demonic cases, I would have been fascinated to see if there were measurable changes in the temperature that correlated with our blessing.

We started our way up the stairs to the main floor and I could sense that the entity had not yet released its grasp on the home and family. "How is it down there?" Kacey asked.

I still had to finish blessing the whole main level of the house but it felt a lot better. I reassured her that I was seeing positive results and that the entity was weakening. I was amazed to see that Holly was still fast asleep in Shannon's arms despite the unsettling experience Shannon had while we were in the basement. Sometimes I really do believe God or angelic spirits protect the children during a blessing.

After opening all the closets and doors, I made my way through the kitchen, the bathrooms, bedrooms, and finally into Shannon's bedroom. Carl and I each chose separate corners to begin blessing when we heard a peculiar sound—a low, deep rumble. I glanced around to see what the disturbance was, only to find that Shannon's dresser was vibrating.

Carl and I both stopped our movements to make sure the floorboards were not causing the commotion. The vibrating continued. I walked over to the dresser and began praying over it while my hand was placed on top. After a minute of time had passed, the rumbling subsided as if an engine were slowly coming to a halt. We resumed blessing the bedroom and prayed that there would not be any further distractions in hopes of finally finishing the ceremony.

As if on cue, I finished reciting the last of the prayers when I felt the darkness lift from the home. I felt as if the house breathed a sigh of relief and a black sheet was pulled off of the roof. Maybe the white sage was getting to my senses, but everything seemed brighter again and more vivid. The euphoria present in the home was overpowering and I felt as relaxed and smooth as room-temperature butter (real organic butter, not margarine).

"Well, there you have it!" we laughed. God's light and love poured in through the windows and doors of the home like a warm ocean wave washing over the family, healing their cuts and wounds.

Great Spirit's power never ceases to amaze me. After experiencing such intense encounters with the dark, I will never deny that there is a God. I hope that you, too, will consider the unseen world and that there are never coincidences, and everything is meant to happen for a reason—for a lesson.

After holding a closing prayer and giving thanks with the family, I went about the usual routine of packing away my supplies and belongings. Now that I had finished my rounds with their demon, I had to return home to face my own demons…homework and writing a thesis.

The last time I spoke with Kacey, she said that her home had finally returned to normal and they were no longer experiencing paranormal encounters of any kind. I sent information and techniques for Kacey to use in order to protect herself while at work in the cemetery. Shannon's attitude improved greatly and their disputes returned to a minimal level. Holly is now living in a safe and loving home and my mind and heart have been put to rest. I hope their lives continue to improve and that they are never plagued by darkness again.

CHAPTER 6

TAYLOR, MICHIGAN CASE
—INCUBUS/SUCCUBUS

Not all hauntings are successfully removed. Sometimes it takes repeated attempts to cast out an entity. Other times the clients or the parties involved give up for various reasons. For whatever reason, the battle against the dark is lost and resolution is not found. This is one of those cases, and I still am haunted by the lack of closure.

In June of 2009 a distraught woman contacted me about a haunting she and her family were experiencing. Clarissa was a mother of four and a wife to Rick; they had recently married each other after leaving previous spouses. Clarissa asked me where she could find white sage smudging supplies as she intended to perform a house cleansing. She stated that she wanted to remove a negative spirit from her home and wondered if I knew of any stores nearby that carried the supplies.

I gave her some references and advice and told her to let me know how her cleansing went. I had taught many individuals how to remove hauntings and to cleanse their homes with much success. Clarissa seemed ambitious and strong enough to properly conduct a cleansing, so I had considerable faith in her efforts.

Two weeks later I sent her a follow-up e-mail to see how the cleansing went and if she still needed help. I never heard from her again until seven months later in January of 2010. I was surprised to receive her second e-mail; so much time had passed since we last spoke. I had assumed that everything had gone well and she did not need any further help. I was wrong.

It seems like it's getting stronger, she wrote. Clarissa explained that another paranormal group from the area had attempted to perform a cleansing, which they botched, and on several later occasions the group stood the family up. The activity flared up and more damage was done at the hands of the in-experienced group.

Clarissa mentioned that Rick would anoint the headboard in the sign of the cross every night with holy water, only to be tormented by horrible nightmares. They sought assistance from their family's church but received little help other than an invitation to join in on the church services.

One morning Clarissa spoke to the entity in her home and sarcastically said, "See you in church!" After attending Mass that day, she awoke later with a temperature of 104.6 degrees Fahrenheit and became violently ill for a long period, without a viable rationalization from the doctors. Clarissa sought more outside help; she contacted priests, but they were reluctant to assist.

I could sense her frustration. I am disappointed in the lack of assistance from many churches these days. Very few ministries are willing to help and I feel they have forgotten their obligations to the public and God. Clarissa had exhausted every possible route aside from bringing in an exorcist.

Clarissa's youngest daughter Cally reported seeing moving shadows in her room at night and a "catlike figure"—a small, black creature with eyes like a feline. I knew I was not dealing with a typical human spirit. This was something more sinister.

Clarissa was exhausted and wanted this entity removed. She wrote that she hadn't slept much in almost a year. Clarissa's employer was becoming aggravated with how much work she was missing and she was always severely fatigued on the job. Even her coworkers began to think she was crazy after overhearing her talk about the entity.

Clarissa was desperate for help and felt very alone. I worried for Clarissa and Rick, and especially for their young children, and wanted to pursue this case immediately. First I had to ask the previous paranormal group several questions about the cleansing they performed and find out what exactly went wrong. Unbeknownst to me, I walked into a political and territorial scene in the paranormal community.

I was taken aback to find out that some paranormal groups are unfortunately working on behalf of lower ambitions. These groups seem to be set on acquiring as many cases as possible, fame and thrills—forgetting that their primary objective should be helping the clients. The paranormal group I contacted still felt they had "rights" to the case despite not returning phone calls to Clarissa, ignoring her for many months, conducting a failed cleansing, and making matters worse. I never intrude on another group's case, but it was clear they had put this case on the back burner or had given up.

Clarissa made it very clear to me that she wished to no longer associate with that group and that she welcomed my help. I relayed the message to the previous group and subsequently received many confused and harassing e-mails from them. The leader greatly struggled with comprehending that Clarissa resigned their group from the case. Trying to remain professional, and keeping the goal of helping Clarissa in mind, I ended communications with the group. I was given little information and walked away from the situation more confused than I was before talking with them. It was useless but a good lesson learned.

With all the political drama behind me, I could now continue with scheduling a blessing for Clarissa and her family.

She wrote: *"P.S. I think it can read our thoughts. Is that possible?"*

Although Clarissa described a very powerful entity in our discussions, I was not prepared to hear the horrific details upon meeting with the family. It was surreal.

On February 12, 2010, Carl and I prepared to perform our afternoon cleansing for Clarissa's home. I was drying my hair in our bathroom that morning when I witnessed something not of this world. I had flipped my hair upside down and was brushing through it when some movement in the corner caught my eye. I looked into our living room area and saw what was at least a seven-foot-tall entity dart across the room. It was black, lanky, and moved at an incredible speed.

My heart raced as I threw down the hair dryer. I ran into the living room. I spun around, looking about the room. *Nothing was there.* I somehow found my voice through the violation I felt. "Get the hell out of my house! You are not welcome here! Whether you like it or not, we're still coming to do the cleansing! You're not going to scare me off!" I yelled as if I were kicking a drunk out of a bar. I looked outside the kitchen window and saw Carl with my two English Bulldogs by the garage.

I opened the screen door and called to Carl. "A seven-foot-tall demon just flew through our freaking living room!" I'm grateful our neighbor didn't hear my wild accusations. I had never seen anything like it before.

Carl became upset that it had visited me in our home, trying to ward me off from performing the day's cleansing. I felt safe in the rental home, whether it was actually protected or not, and having a demon visit *inside* the home immediately tossed that idea right out the window. The Bulldogs, Jack and Annabelle, of course had no idea what had just happened and were content with chewing away on their toys and soon drifted off to sleep. I am glad that neither Carl nor the dogs had to experience what I saw—it was truly disturbing. After regaining my composure, I continued getting ready and was soon prepared to leave. *Another strange morning.*

We arrived at Clarissa's house earlier than expected and pulled up to the condominium home. I like to play a "first impressions game" in which I try to psychically pick up on the home and the spirits present before speaking with the clients.

"How do you feel, Carl?" I asked inquisitively.

"I feel … amorous," Carl said with confusion. I didn't realize until later how foreshadowing that comment was in regards to the nature of the case.

Carl and I met with Clarissa's husband Rick to figure out how and why the entity had come into their lives. Clarissa was away at work, but during her lunch break she was able to come home for a half hour to talk with us briefly. During the discussion and interview, I was told that Clarissa's ex-husband was familiar with the dark arts and had performed Santeria hexes before. After reviewing the possible causes of the presence, I theorized that her ex-husband had sent her a demonic entity in retaliation after learning that Clarissa was getting remarried. In fact, following the notice of the upcoming marriage, her ex-husband sent her a text message reading, "Die." Shortly after, Clarissa and Rick began experiencing the entity in their home. It seemed more than coincidental.

I recorded the interview on my digital voice recorder for documentation reasons, not fully expecting that I would capture a very disturbing EVP. Rick had been talking about how I should try lying down on their master bed, like the previous paranormal group did, to experience the inappropriate touching of the entity. The entity seemed to enjoy the idea of me laying on the bed and wanted to encourage me to participate.

The EVP entails a sleazy and cunning male voice saying, "Sweetheart, try this, won't you?" This was directly in response to when Rick discussed the touching on the bed at the time the EVP was recorded.

I never did lie on the bed but instead pushed forward with the interview and cleansing. After later hearing the EVP I was glad I didn't participate in the "bed experiment." I never want to give an entity an advantage or a way to manipulate me—I had to stay on track with my objective to remove the demon.

As I sat there taking notes about the case, I was mortified to find out that the entity was sexually assaulting and raping Clarissa and Rick. They had never mentioned anything this severe in their e-mail and I was a bit shocked. Now I understood why Carl was picking up on the sexual nature of the case when I asked him his first impression, and I wonder if this same entity influenced Carl long after the case.

I had read numerous case studies in which victims were being sexually harassed, but it was entirely different to hear these clients share the same experiences right in front of me. They described a telepathic connection with the entity in which they would mentally instruct the entity to perform a certain sexual act. As if reading their minds, the demon would follow the instructions precisely. "We thought it was funny at first," Clarissa explained. "We thought it was just some horny ghost." As the "fun and games" progressed, eventually they were forcefully penetrated and raped by the entity. It was finally showing its true colors.

Interestingly enough, the entity seemed to switch between sexes depending on whom it was presenting itself to.

If it was molesting Rick, the entity would have female characteristics such as breasts and a vagina. If it was molesting Clarissa, the entity would have a distinct penis and male genitals. My stomach sank as I realized we were dealing with an incubus and a succubus.

On a quick side note, I actually believe that this incubus and succubus could be the same entity. Demons are well-known for shape shifting and manifesting themselves into various illusions—why couldn't it simply change sexes depending on which victim it was harassing? We have numerous organisms on this earth that can change sexes; perhaps the same phenomena exists in the paranormal world. Also, Clarissa and Rick were never assaulted at the same time, thus leading me to believe there was only *one* entity performing the sexual acts at any given time. The only thing preventing me from fully accepting this theory for this case was that there were two distinct male and female voices captured as an EVP during my interview with Clarissa and Rick. However, for the sake of writing I will simply refer to the incubus and succubus as one entity in this story.

During this discussion the digital voice recorder picked up another EVP of a female voice, panting and moaning in a sexual manner, followed by her saying, "It's a job." As if the succubus's sexual harassment and raping was something it considered being a job and a chore. Years later I wondered if the entity actually said "Izajasz," which is a birth name that means "God is salvation." Demons seem to love to mock the holy and divine, so it would be fitting and in poor taste—something demons excel at.

In the back of my mind I felt that Rick may have been having an extra-marital affair; however, I could have been sensing the private sexual relationship he shared with the succubus. The sexual connection Clarissa and Rick had with the entity would be enough to cause a deep rift in their marriage—just as a third-party affair would cause. It was completely unhealthy for their relationship and now the entity was destroying the couple's trust and faith in each other.

As with many of the cases mentioned in this book, there are numerous ways to break down the trust and structure of a family or relationship. In this particular case, the demon chose to use humankind's sexual desire against Clarissa and Rick to gain a hold on their lives. What started off as just pure sexual behavior soon turned into violent rapes and assaults, proving that demons will often first appear as something entirely different and innocent, then turn more sinister.

As we sat talking with Rick and Clarissa, their small Maltese dog began barking and growling. Sitting in the dining room chair, I had my back to the dog and the couch it sat on. Slowly, the dog began climbing up the couch and perched itself on the highest part, sniffing the air and growling. When we first arrived the dog was very friendly towards us and I gave it lots of affection. Now, it leaned forward and began inspecting the back of my neck. At the same time, I felt the evil presence of the demon come into the room. I believe the entity then stood close to me, trying to bait the dog towards me in an angry manner—perhaps trying to startle me.

"It's here," Carl stated.

Rick and Clarissa both confirmed that they also felt a change in the room. I sat there calmly, figuring that the demon was likely stirring up trouble, waiting for a reaction and trying to distract us. Clarissa scolded the dog and eventually it returned to its spot on the couch. I was slightly concerned that the dog would try to bite my neck and was happy to see it retire to the sofa.

I finished my long interview with Clarissa and Rick and decided it was time to proceed with the house blessing. Clarissa had to return to work, as she was already running late from her lunch break. I was sad to see her leave, but she hoped to return from work later in the evening to a changed home—a peaceful and relaxing place for her family to live.

I gathered my supplies and asked Rick to prepare the rooms in the house by opening the windows and closets with us. I unpacked my materials and handed Rick several holy anointing oils for them to keep, in addition to a holy candle. I told him to burn the candle whenever he felt disturbed and to use the oil to anoint themselves and their rooms. Rick was very appreciative and put the items in a safe place until the blessing was finished.

I could feel the pressure building in the home and knew that I would either be confronted by the demon or it would hide.

I was a bit hesitant given the fact that this home was a condominium. In my opinion, attached or adjoining homes, like condominiums, are more difficult to cleanse because you can't fully bless the entire building, thus the entities can simply move to another unit temporarily and return later to haunt once the blessing is finished. I was concerned about not having access to the other units. It was impossible to go around "blessing" everyone's unit in a condominium! Likely I would end up in a psychiatric ward. *There's that weird girl trying to cast out demons again!* No thank you.

As we began blessing the home we first started from the front door to the back of the house and out towards the sliding door. The Maltese seemed to be comforted by the white sage aroma and soon settled down comfortably on its bed. "That feels better, right?" I sweetly asked the dog. We ascended the stairs towards the kids' bedrooms and I saw a chinchilla in a cage in the hallway. We later found out it was named Chinchy. It frantically raced about the enclosure and seemed on edge. The entire house seemed to be on pins and needles; I admittedly felt a bit jumpy as well. This was one of the most bizarre and disturbing cases I had dealt with.

The bedroom of the oldest daughter, Nicole, felt very dense and oppressed. I sensed that the demon spent a lot of time in this room, or was currently present in the room with me. We worked our way through the rooms and into the parents' bedroom. I also sensed the same dark feeling in the master bedroom, a thick negativity loomed.

I usually record the counseling sessions with the client for documentation. On this occasion, the digital recorder had been recording the entire time we performed the house blessing. An unusual low, deep rumble was heard on the recorder when I began the smudging part of the ceremony; it seemed to have an effect on the entity.

I felt there was a connection with the attic space and the bedrooms, as if the entity used the attic as an entrance or place to hide, so we asked Rick if we could borrow a ladder to access the attic. I always bless the attics, basements, crawl spaces, and so on, but wanted to address this area immediately so the entity couldn't seek refuge there during the rest of the blessing.

As Carl braced the ladder, he lifted the door to the attic and I balanced behind him with the abalone shell and white sage smudging supplies. Suddenly, the abalone shell became unbearably hot; I felt the jolt of pain and nearly dropped the shell. It began burning my hands so I had to find an alternative way for me to continue holding the shell. Rick offered an oven mitt, which proved to be very helpful.

As we continued with the blessing of the attic we began to notice a terrible burning smell stirring through the air. Many demonic entities will manifest odors and foul smells, so I wasn't completely surprised when I caught a whiff of something like burning rubber. However, the smell became so strong none of us could ignore it.

During this time Carl was holding the abalone shell with the oven mitt. I finally realized that the oven mitt was starting to burn from the abalone shell! The smoldering white sage was *so* hot that it was burning through the thick abalone shell and into the mitt beneath it. I had *never* seen this before—something burning through several dense layers. I think it was apparent that the entity was trying to prevent us from continuing with our cleansing.

Then the phones began to ring, their home phone and our cell phones, at different times but all in succession of each other. Other distractions followed and we eventually unplugged the house phones and turned off our cell phones. I explained to Rick that this was pretty common; entities would try all sorts of methods to get us to stop the cleansing. I refocused my efforts and continued on with my mission.

Carl began anointing the home with olive oil and I made my rounds with the salt. For some reason the entity didn't seem to be completely gone—just weakened. This lingering presence really bothered me and I began kneeling and praying in Nicole's room. I was desperate. *"God, please help this family find peace. Cast out any demons and evils that reside in this home. There are innocent children in this home and they need to be protected. They need your help. I know that they let their guard down and unknowingly bonded with a demon, but I really think they're ready to have the entity removed. Please help me cast out this evil and bring them closer to you. In your name I pray forever and ever. Amen."*

I continued with praying and commanding the entity out and I felt its energy weaken, to the point where I was unsure if it still was in the house or not. I held my breath and waited. I had performed so many house blessings that I had become desensitized to the feeling of when an entity finally leaves. *Was the entity still there, just in hiding?* In my heart I was worried that the incubus hadn't left, but I wanted to remain positive and give the blessing a chance to work. Maybe I was just being paranoid and the blessing was fine. I was hesitant to put away the supplies and to end the ceremony, but we had performed all the steps and needed to talk further with Rick.

I still felt suspicious…

We sat down with Rick, as I usually do with clients after a blessing, and asked him to recite some commands and prayers with us. We thoroughly denounced all involvement with the dark and prayed that any hexes placed upon the family would be abolished. I asked Rick if he'd like to share any other comments. He began telling the demon to leave their home, "Get out of here! We don't want you here anymore and you need to leave! Leave us alone!"

Sometimes it serves as therapy for clients to be able to speak their minds and to demand that the entities leave. Rick said he felt better and confirmed that the house seemed more peaceful.

"Let me know if the entity does come back and I will return to do another cleansing or I can begin to apply for an ordained deliverance," I told him. Rick was content and I prayed deeply that the family would finally be at peace.

As I began packing my our supplies, the children returned from school and were quite inquisitive about what we were doing and why the house "smelled funny." Nicole seemed skeptical and slightly annoyed with our visit, waiting to be allowed to watch TV once we had left their house. I pet the Maltese goodbye and we were on our way home. I felt drained but also excited that we had completed another blessing for a family, hoping that it was the solution they needed.

While driving back, I noticed a massive bird flying above the tree line, which I assumed was a turkey vulture. Upon closer examination, I realized it was a bald eagle. I hoped it was a sign from God that we had successfully helped the family, but I also view eagles and hawks as a message for "beware or be aware."

Even though I was exhausted, I had trouble sleeping that night and thoughts of Clarissa and her family kept racing through my mind. I sent her an e-mail before bed asking her to let me know how everything went and to notify me if the demon troubled them any further. I just hoped it really worked.

In the following days I checked my mail continuously and finally found a message from Clarissa several days after the blessing. The news was not good. The entity had returned the night after the cleansing. It was my worst fear. We had severely upset the entity and Clarissa said it was one of the worst nights they had experienced—everyone was poked, touched, and harassed during the night. They also had nightmares. In retrospect, I wish I had stayed the night with the family to help protect them.

This entity was a coward—instead of confronting us while we were there, it waited until the family was alone at night and vulnerable. The children were never told about the nature of our visit and their violent experiences that night confirmed that something paranormal was happening; it was not just mass hysteria.

The night after the cleansing, all the children began sharing their experiences. Clarissa was horrified to learn that Nicole was being sexually assaulted by the entity and had been for quite some time. *"She just thought it was her body behaving*

weird, until she described her experiences and I realized she was
encountering the same raping that I was! She's only fifteen and a
virgin so she doesn't understand!"

My heart was heavy reading Clarissa's e-mail. I wish the
children had spoken up sooner so we could have addressed
the haunting fully and had them present for the blessing.

I was disappointed, worried, and angry. I felt that I let the
family down. I was concerned for their immediate well-being
and I was entirely furious with the demon. Our blessing did
something to wound the demon and it was rebelling, trying
to punish the family again for seeking help, much as it did
whenever they tried to go to church.

As with the most severe hauntings, some cases require
multiple blessings and exorcisms, depending on the entity's
strength and level of attachment. This entity had embedded
itself so deeply by having a sexual relationship with the family.
I had never dealt with a case that required a second blessing,
but knew that I couldn't abandon the family.

I began contacting different churches and ministers in
hopes of a resolution. *No one* was willing to help.

Finally, I came across one of the few exorcists in Michigan,
B.T. Hubbard (fictional name). I had previously attended one
of his seminars on demonology. Although we didn't completely see eye-to-eye on religious matters, I figured he would
be able to help the family. This case would prove to be a learning experience on several levels.

I asked Pastor Hubbard if he could help with the case.
Because Nicole was now reportedly being raped by the entity,
it was critical to me that the family received immediate help.

Clarissa was nearly hysterical. I had not heard a response from Pastor Hubbard and put more pressure on him to tend to the case as soon as he could. I was deeply concerned for the family and my heart and soul was tied into the case. I wanted to protect and save them in any way possible.

It took Hubbard over eight weeks to visit with the family. Prior to his visit, Hubbard stated that in order to perform an exorcism or deliverance, he required solid evidence. I immediately sent him the EVPs I captured during our visit, but he insisted he required more unyielding evidence. He requested that a paranormal group he worked with visit and perform an investigation at Clarissa's house. I had no problem with bringing in another group, however, I viewed it as unnecessary stalling. The family was at their wit's end and was close to crumbling apart; I wanted to act quickly.

I insisted that the demonic entity was real and ever-present in the family's home. For weeks Clarissa tried contacting Hubbard but was often left without a response. Finally, after reviewing the evidence from his paranormal team's appointment and client testimonials, Hubbard's verdict came in and we were in agreement that this truly was a demonic case. He claimed, "Incubi and succubi are the hardest to get rid of."

I still prayed that he would be able to help the family. *Maybe these things just take time.* I was desperate to find the family any kind of help as long as it would bring them peace and happiness.

Weeks passed and Clarissa contacted me very upset after Hubbard had made his visit for a deliverance. During his stay there, Clarissa was informed that the demon was primarily her fault because she occasionally read daily horoscopes. "I am not so sure about his beliefs of us being so sinful just because I read a horoscope," Clarissa shared. Clarissa felt condemned by Hubbard and sobbed during much of his visit. She was made to believe that the demonic haunting was her fault. She felt intense guilt and sadness; her entire family was suffering and her own daughter was being raped as a result of her mother's actions.

My theory that Clarissa's ex-husband had sent her the entity after their divorce—the "die" text message and his experience with practicing black magic—was not considered. In Hubbard's mind, the culprit was the daily horoscopes.

I followed up with Clarissa again and asked if she felt a difference in the home since Hubbard's visit. She stated she felt his visit might have been helpful but was unsure of her personal experience with Hubbard, "… *I don't know if he is living in 2011; things are different since biblical times. LOL.*" I was glad that Clarissa was able to find some humor and light out of the experience with Hubbard. I really hoped his exorcism worked and that Clarissa was finally at peace.

I checked with Clarissa a month later to see if progress had been made and discovered that the entity was *still* residing in the home. *How was this possible?* The deliverance Hubbard performed had failed. In Hubbard's defense, I will say that sometimes if a client is not committed to changing himself or herself for the better, to stop involving themselves in negative habits and behaviors, that the entity will likely not leave. I felt that Clarissa and her family were very committed to removing the entity, but despite their best efforts it remained in their home. I was unsure as to why the exorcism failed and felt that we were facing a brick wall without any more routes or options to choose from.

On June 2, 2010 Clarissa wrote me back, *"It still lingers … rainy days bring out the worst, but we are surviving."*

I kept in contact with Clarissa for quite some time to make sure the presence was no longer physically attacking the family and offered to find additional help from the church. However, I was happy to hear that when Clarissa would unplug the electronics and appliances, the entity was weakened and rarely caused problems. Finally, after a blessing and deliverance, the solution seemed to be electrical and unorthodox. It was the resolution we all had been waiting for.

Entities sometimes take a while to release their grasp on a family, and I prayed that if they prevented the demon from feeding off energy it would eventually leave. Many, many months passed and I hadn't heard from Clarissa. In my mind the family had started a new chapter and regained a happy life. No response was a good thing.

Although I believed that the family had reclaimed their lives for the better, this case had always remained under my skin. It was the one case that resulted in an unsuccessful house blessing and I would often find myself wondering about the family and pondering why the blessings failed. I had dealt with equally severe cases and had great success with casting out the demons … *why didn't this one work?* It stumped me.

I had many months to consider why the cleansing failed and concluded on several reasons or theories. One was that in our rushed efforts to get the family the help they deserved, we scheduled a house blessing on a day the children were at school. Clarissa was able to stop in during her lunch break and Rick was at the home with us the entire time.

I later deeply regretted this last-minute decision. However, this also led me to change the way I currently perform house cleansings. I now require *all* family members to be present during the cleansing and to remain present until the cleansing is finished. A large part of battling the demonic involves the family acting as a whole unit, a team, and working together. Also, an entity can jump to locations to hide with one of the family members until the cleansing is finished and return home to the family to continue its haunting. By having all the members together, a bond is built in the family and the entity doesn't have an escape route.

In Clarissa's family's case, having children present at the cleansing would have allowed them to share their experiences, such as Nicole's assaults, and further bring closure to the family. Instead, the cleansing was performed and after the fact the children were able to come forward. When Clarissa and Rick learned of the children's attacks, it only fueled fear and negative emotions. There was much emotional unrest after the cleansing, which may have altered the results and left a good foothold for the demon to remain attached to the family.

Another mistake we made was networking with several individuals who claimed to be experienced with demonic cases and entities. At one point, I had recruited the help of a colleague, John M., who claimed to have experience with demonic cases. John joined us for Clarissa's house blessing. Despite our long and thorough discussion about the seriousness of the case and what the blessing would entail, I was later disturbed to find out that John was interested in performing hexes and so on.

While interviewing Clarissa and Rick during our visit, John was present and mentioned how he was "tempted to hex a person a few weeks ago." I almost had a heart attack. He never mentioned anything of that matter during our conversation and I felt embarrassed and deceived to be in the presence of someone like that. Likely he was there for thrills and may have also led to the failure of the cleansing.

During a cleansing, everyone present must be on the same page with only one goal in mind: to help the family. If you are in the presence of someone with lower ambitions, such as hexing others, their energy may also cause the blessing to fail. I shared my deep apologizes with the family and no longer associate with either John or Hubbard.

Needless to say, I no longer bring in inexperienced individuals or "newbies." If I feel I need support, only Mike and a few others will join me to perform house cleansings. Our energies and methods work very well together and I'm happy with our technique. Not only is bringing in an inexperienced individual a liability for safety of the family, but the newcomer is also at risk of being harmed. This was another possible reason as to why the house blessing failed, but I will never know for sure.

I wasn't present for the deliverance or exorcism, so I wasn't sure as to why Hubbard's attempt failed. *How was it that two experienced groups, Hubbard and ourselves, were unable to help Clarissa?* Perhaps this was just a difficult case and I would be left wondering for the rest of my life—something I didn't want to accept. *Everyone can be helped and saved.* Maybe I was being naïve from the beginning.

At least, I thought, Clarissa had found a way to starve the demon of its energy and the family had found a solution. But then I heard back from Clarissa.

On December 12, 2011, a year and a half later, I received an e-mail from a familiar address:

> *"I am still having issues. I just thought you might want to know, Samantha. Rick and I are currently separated and we left the house. But it is still with me every night. I don't sleep at all. Doc has me on sleeping pills. My hair is super gray now too. I keep having to dye it. I don't know what to do."*

I sat there reading the e-mail from Clarissa and I became deeply saddened. I had often said prayers to God that He helped Clarissa and her family, just in case they were still experiencing the entity. Now it was confirmed they were still being haunted. This damned entity wanted to take her life and soul, that was apparent. It would be convenient to just kill or get into a good old-fashioned bar fight with a demon; however, it's not that easy. Demons are persistent and conniving.

Clarissa and I began talking eagerly again. I suggested that I perform another house blessing. Since the original blessing, I had come to incorporate a more potent method of cleansing houses and felt very confident that this technique would work. Clarissa appreciated the offer but felt that the house was no longer haunted; instead, she felt that she, herself, was haunted. "It is very strong now. Much stronger than before. I really believe it possesses my body at night...My head gets heavy and I fall into a deep sleep. When I try to wake and try to get it off of me it holds me down and won't let me speak or move."

The entity had grown in strength, as many do, over the time it was attached to the family. "The other day really scared me; I said a prayer out loud and did the cross where it was strongest (near my neck) and just then its claws grabbed at my hand to knock it away. It was fierce. It was very strong. And I literally felt claws."

Clarissa was experiencing strange health problems that appeared out of nowhere and correlated with the beginning of the haunting. I instructed Clarissa to perform a few protection rituals until I was able to help further with a different blessing. Christmas, New Year's, and Clarissa's birthday were coming up and she wasn't sure when she could schedule another blessing. I told her to contact me immediately when she was ready for a blessing and sent her some special prayers to recite until my visit.

"You truly inspire me. I just got home from the hospital so I just saw your email today. One thing is for sure, I said the prayer out loud a few times and my entire body tingled from the top of my head down to my feet. It was a little strange. So I am not sure if that is normal or whether it is surrounding me. Very odd feeling...My kids had to take me to the hospital because my legs were completely swollen (ankles and feet too)...I was dizzy and pale as a ghost. They ran some tests on my heart. They think I might have acute

heart failure. Yes, I am only thirty-nine. I have VERY high blood pressure and rapid heartbeat. My heart is beating at 137 per minute when it is supposed to only be at ninety to one hundred."

The entity seemed to be claiming Clarissa's body and health—her willingness to fight was dwindling.

"Ever since we have been having issues with this THING I have been in and out of the hospital. So far: kidney stones, gall bladder, appendicitis, and now acute heart failure … On top of it all the stress with the family and work-related things are driving me completely insane."

Although Clarissa felt that a house blessing would only cleanse a home, I reassured her that it also removes the negative energy and spirit from a person.

"The bags under my eyes are black and swollen from no sleep. It is just not healthy. I feel sick all the time. I stopped talking about it to people because they just think I am crazy or I am paranoid and hallucinating. Boy, I wish I were!"

I finally contacted Lorraine Warren. She and her late husband are famous demonologists, and I highly valued her opinion on how to handle an incubus/succubus case. I remember dialing her phone number, unsure as to what to expect but with great excitement as I had always admired her. The phone rang a few times and I recognized her sweet voice on the other end of the line.

I introduced myself and asked if she had time for a few questions.

"Hold on, honey! Just a second!" Lorraine began to violently cough. I got really nervous, hoping that Lorraine was all right. I felt helpless listening to this wonderful and elderly woman fighting to get a breath. *Oh please don't die on me, Lorraine!* I thought to myself as I suggested that she hang up the phone and call for help if needed. It seemed as if minutes had passed as I sat there listening in horror. The paranormal community would probably never forgive me if my phone call led to her passing.

"My goodness! I was choking on my orange juice!" Lorraine exclaimed as she cleared her throat.

"Oh my gosh! Are you okay now? I got so worried!" We laughed together a bit and I remember hearing her chickens clucking in the background—a woman after my own heart.

I really appreciated her insight and the time she took to talk with me. We share a lot of the same opinions and theories on hauntings and her life experience is awe-inspiring.

"The phone is always ringing! Every fifteen minutes!" Poor Lorraine was taking phone calls from strangers and colleagues constantly. She has dedicated her life to helping so many people and treading where others refuse to go. It was truly an honor to talk with her.

I explained Clarissa's case to her and how the blessing and deliverance had both failed. She explained that she would be in Toronto for a lecture in a month and suggested that I meet her for lunch. "Oh, Lorraine, I would be honored!" And so we planned to meet in Canada.

But then I realized my passport was expired and I began scrambling to obtain an enhanced driver's license that would allow me to cross the border by car without a passport. The Secretary of State clerk informed me that it would take over six weeks to get the ID in the mail. I paid for a "rush order" of the ID and prayed that it would arrive in time. *Well, I could get into Canada easily ... getting back into the U.S. without my passport or enhanced ID would be difficult.*

Weeks passed and nothing arrived in the mail. I grew anxious, fearing that I wouldn't be able to attend my lunch with Lorraine. I had always wanted to meet her. She was one of the few people that I looked up to in this world. She had dealt with some of the most severe cases and her insight could help resolve Clarissa's case. I informed Clarissa that I would be discussing matters with Lorraine in hopes of finding her a final solution. Until then, I had to continue to wait.

One day I received a call from the owner and manager of the Holly Hotel. She asked me if I would be able to host an episode of *Most Terrifying Places in America* for the Travel Channel in the upcoming weeks. I happily agreed as I was very familiar with the history of the place and had numerous personal experiences while I was at the Holly Hotel. I would host annual "ghost hunts" at the Holly Hotel and lots of people witnessed the paranormal during their visits.

As the days approached toward my meeting with Lorraine in Canada, I realized that my passport and enhanced ID would not arrive in the mail in time. I regretfully wrote a message to

Lorraine informing her that I wouldn't be able to attend our planned lunch and thanked her continuously for the generous offer. Lorraine made several recommendations on how to handle the case and the entity. Unfortunately, it became a moot point during this phase of the haunting as I had already tried everything she suggested. Lorraine didn't know of any references for me in the Michigan area that I could contact for help. We were out of ideas and options. I felt as if I hit a brick wall. I now had to turn my focus back on Clarissa and to find her the help she needed.

Despite facing a dead-end situation with Clarissa's case, I still had an obligation to film with the Travel Channel that weekend. I was distracted while filming, as thoughts of Clarissa rolled around in my head and I constantly pondered, *What do I do now?* I wish sometimes that God would communicate with us via a large billboard sign that would clearly state how to handle dire situations like this. I just wanted to help but I didn't know how.

Clarissa emailed me in December of 2011 and we aimed to schedule an additional blessing after her birthday in January. Finally, a response and an estimated timeline! I asked her to send me some dates that would work for her and I would visit as soon as I heard back from her. By this time, the entity had killed their chinchilla, Chinchy, the dog's health was in decline, and, of course, Clarissa had separated from Rick. It seemed as though the entity was succeeding in its mission to destroy the family's life. Chomping at the bit, I was ready to perform a blessing again. But, I *never* heard back from Clarissa again. Nothing. That was it.

In my deepest fears, I worried that Clarissa had given in to the entity, that she was struggling in the hospital, or that it finally took her life. I made *relentless* attempts to contact Clarissa, only to find no response or that the phone numbers were disconnected. I no longer knew her home address as she had moved into a new condominium, so I couldn't drop by to check in on her.

Clarissa and I shared a close enough connection that if she had been uncomfortable or unsure of the upcoming blessing in any way, she would have let me know. I couldn't imagine her just blocking my number and ignoring my e-mails. *What happened to her?*

Clarissa had been in and out of the hospital and I worried that her health took a turn for the worse. Maybe the entity was aware of my upcoming visit and decided to hurry its efforts. I searched through the Taylor obituaries and held my breath. I was grateful her name was absent from the list.

I could have written an entire book about all of my successes with casting out demons and glorifying all the families I have helped; however, I wanted to share my failures as well. Although I would never seek to blame one person or one reason alone for a failed case, it's important to acknowledge that the paranormal never goes according to plan. Hence, why it is considered "paranormal."

I always respect a client's personal life and space, so I let them contact me on their own terms. I never want to be forceful or impose myself on a client. Throughout this case I always told Clarissa to contact me immediately if they needed help and, on occasion, I would check in with her on my own efforts. Perhaps I gave Clarissa too much space; maybe I should have been more pressing with her. Then again, I could drive myself nuts feeling that I "didn't do enough." I had contacted numerous churches, clergy, an exorcist, other demonologists, and I gave it my personal best shot.

Clarissa's communication was always irregular, sometimes months or years would pass until I heard from her, despite my best efforts at getting her to respond. If I ever heard back from Clarissa asking for a house blessing, I would visit her in a heartbeat and return to remove the entity with a vengeance. Perhaps I will hear from her again soon.

Likely, Clarissa will always haunt my memories. I pray she and her family are finally at peace. As much as this chapter leaves you feeling unsatisfied and needing closure, I, too, feel disturbed by the lack of resolution.

I apologize to my readers for dragging them into a chapter without an apparent ending, but there was much to learn from this story. Now we can ponder "what happened to Clarissa" together. This is the realistic side of the paranormal. Sometimes there is no answer or happily ever after ending. And that is something I still have a hard time accepting.

CHAPTER 7

NEW BALTIMORE, MICHIGAN CASE

In dealing with paranormal cases, not everything is as it seems. Taking a scientific and skeptical approach is important and sometimes there are rational explanations to be had. Now and then the "bizarre" is a product of the living and not an otherworldly experience.

Josh was a retired engineer and a Vietnam veteran. He and his wife, Kathy, lived in a quaint condominium in New Baltimore, Michigan. In January of 2012 their case was forwarded on to me from another paranormal group. We were the seventh group to try to assist Kathy and Josh in their severe haunting. In addition to the previous paranormal teams, Kathy had also enlisted the help of two Catholic priests, one pastor, and a psychic. It seemed as though Kathy had exhausted every route possible to removing their haunting.

I came into contact with Kathy through two individuals who desired to start their own paranormal team but were still in the start-up phase. Jason, the leader, was previously part of another paranormal group, and his new partner Matt was approximately nineteen years old and managed the networking and communications of their small group. They were eager to find cases, gather evidence, and dive into the world of the paranormal.

I began receiving frequent contact from Matt, which eventually evolved into a short bought of stalking, full of daily phone calls and other socially awkward situations. I felt hesitant about how the case would continue to unfold. Matt proposed the concept of calling me every day after Christmas. He was a sweet soul but I felt I was being held hostage via my phone's cell tower during our conversations. I insisted that the focus remain on the case and that I would handle it as soon as possible.

"Well you can cross that off your bucket list, Sam. You officially have your first stalker!" Carl teased and I wasn't appreciative. The paranormal brings all sorts of "weird" into your life—both the living and the dead. With my first mild stalking experience under my belt, I was put in contact with Kathy. However, the case was bound to become even more unusual.

Matt and Jason worked with Kathy first, prior to my involvement in the case. Jason's paranormal group had visited Kathy the evening of February 26 for an investigation and a cleansing ritual. Kathy welcomed the idea of their group blessing her home to remove the demonic entity after being stood up by several other groups. Prior to that evening, however, Jason received six phone calls and voicemails from

Kathy's phone. Apparently the messages consisted of Kathy telling Jason that she didn't want the blessing performed and she no longer needed their help.

Kathy claimed that she never remembered calling Jason. We later hypothesized that the demonic entity was mimicking Kathy's voice and trying to prevent the blessing from ensuing.

Entities had demonstrated this ability in other cases in which the demon disguised its voice as a family member's, so it wasn't that unreasonable of a possibility. Regardless of the phone calls and messages, Jason and his group still appeared at Kathy's house that night.

Jason had recruited the help of an individual named CJ who was experienced with demonic hauntings. CJ was an older man and oddly refused to answer any of Kathy's questions during his visit.

When she asked him if he thought there was more than one demon, he replied, "I don't answer any questions." Kathy found the response unusual, but she felt that they could help her and their blessing proceeded. Kathy watched the ritual through a TV monitor that displayed their security camera's screens. The blessing was to take place in Kathy and Josh's basement, where the demon was likely to reside.

CJ enclosed himself inside a salt circle with symbols for protection as he commanded the demon to leave the house with his crucifix. As Kathy watched in horror, CJ was repeatedly pushed down by the entity. The salt circle didn't seem to protect him from the demon. The ceremony lasted for about half an hour and finally the group determined that the entity had been cast out. After packing up their belongings they bid the family farewell and left.

About a week later I received the initial phone call from Kathy and she felt that the demon was still present in the home. We talked for over an hour. "I first started seeing these balls of light floating around on the walls. Then they kind of turned into black masses." I wrote down Kathy's recollection of the light anomalies.

I questioned whether Kathy was experiencing anything sacrilegious or dark in nature.

"Yes. One night I woke up and saw a full demon staring at the cross above my bed, as if it hated the crucifix. It was about seven or eight feet tall, had green eyes and was wearing a black robe. I think it had a tail." Kathy sounded terrified and although the account seemed extremely detailed for a brief experience I wanted to give her the benefit of the doubt. Perhaps Kathy was dealing with a very powerful demon.

As I went over the timeline of her haunting, I realized that her husband Josh had been diagnosed with cancer around the same time the haunting began. I explained to Kathy that demons are notorious for preying on the weak and the ill—unfortunately, being a cancer patient was a perfect opportunity for such an entity.

I continued asking Kathy about the physical and visual experiences she had in order to get a better grasp on what type of entity she was dealing with. "Every day I see these black angel wings over our bed and they move. What do you think that is?" Kathy inquired.

I explained to Kathy that, in theory, demons are fallen angels and some people report hearing or seeing strange wings. Perhaps she was seeing the demon's wings. Her description puzzled me.

Kathy also reported finding numbers scrawled on the kitchen floor and seeing a demonic figure at the bottom of the stair's landing. She would find footprints leading from the backyard to her door and other prints inside her bedroom closet. In addition to these bizarre events, Kathy would find symbols burned into the grass in their backyard, some of which she recognized.

More than five blessings had been performed on the house. If these other groups and ordained individuals couldn't remove the entity, we would have to perform a very powerful blessing and really work with Josh and Kathy to remove the entity. I wasn't sure if our blessing would make a difference, but we wanted to at least try to help.

I called Mike and asked him if he was available during the upcoming weekend for a blessing on a severe case. By now, Mike had moved to Indiana with his girlfriend and it was difficult to find times when the three of us could all still work together. Eventually, we found a day where Carl, Mike, and I could get together. Mike had to travel over four hours just to get to my house and it was another two hours to Kathy's home in New Baltimore, Michigan.

Surprisingly, I got really good sleep the night before the blessing, and the entire week before we visited I was able to sleep peacefully. I actually found it a bit odd—*why wasn't the demon pestering me like all the other cases?* Maybe it was reserving itself for a battle when we confronted it personally at Kathy's house. Still, I was suspicious.

As we pulled up to Josh and Kathy's house, we didn't experience any strange headaches or physical ailments. I remember thinking to myself *this is also unusual ... no one is being bothered by the entity.* We approached the door and awaited Kathy's reception after ringing the doorbell. I always enjoy seeing what our clients look like after talking on the phone with them for so long. Kathy was in her late sixties or early seventies, short hair, and a small frame. She greeted us and we gathered inside the living room to discuss their haunting and the upcoming blessing.

She had remarkably taken a picture of the entity in her closet and showed us the photograph. Kathy handed me the camera with her frail hands. Her hands gently trembled. I looked over the image on the LCD screen and strained to see the demon that Kathy had captured. Carl, Mike, and I looked over the pictures of the footprints and the apparitions Kathy had photographed.

As he scanned through the images, Carl gave me a sideways glance that I recognized. Something wasn't adding up and Carl was the first to openly acknowledge it. We couldn't find anything paranormal in the pictures.

It wasn't uncommon for people to send me pictures on my website or e-mail claiming they had captured images of ghosts or demons, only to find light reflections, dust, or nothing at all. Pareidolia or "matrixing" is the phenomena in which our brain "identifies" faces in inanimate objects or perceives an image or pattern to be significant when it is truly not. Hence, it's why people believe they see faces in pictures of trees and leaves all the time. Our brains are wired to see faces, so it is hard for some people to realize that it isn't paranormal.

The three of us accepted there was nothing unusual in Kathy's pictures but continued on with the investigation. *Perhaps we would find our own compelling evidence or experiences.*

Kathy began giving us a tour of their home.

"This is our bedroom and where I see the angel's wings above our bed." Kathy pointed.

I was curious about the phenomenon and asked Kathy when she usually sees the wings appear.

"They show up every day, usually around four or five o'clock," she explained. I was shocked. Paranormal activity is rarely this frequent and reliable during a specific time of day. I was constantly learning with each new case, but sometimes the incidents were almost unbelievable. Our tour continued and we headed towards the basement stairs.

"This is where that one tall demon likes to stand. I can see it just faintly right *now*." I stopped dead in my tracks and looked about the room to see the entity Kathy was witnessing. Kathy gestured towards where the demon was standing and I tried to open my sensitivities to perceive it. Despite my efforts, I could *not* see the demon. Kathy was disheartened to find that we didn't see it, like the rest of the investigators who had come through before, and she continued showing us around the house. I had seen shadows and figures occasionally in my years of experience but never as easily as Kathy saw these entities. *Perhaps she was very sensitive and had heightened abilities, but I had my doubts.*

We made our way into the basement and Kathy showed us the location where she could hear growling whenever she recited Psalms from the Bible out loud in the corner. As an experiment, we asked her to begin reading Psalms to see if we could witness the same reaction. I began recording with my digital voice recorder.

Kathy willingly agreed and pulled out her worn Bible. As she began the verses, I closed my eyes and listened closely. I wanted to give Kathy our full attention during the tour before coming to a conclusion. Carl and Mike watched as we all awaited a response from the demon. Several minutes passed and Kathy finally finished reading the section in Psalms. She concluded that the entity must have been hiding. Sometimes entities did hide from us, so not receiving a response from the demon wasn't that uncommon. We continued in the basement until Kathy caught us off guard.

"Do you see its face? It's right there!" she exclaimed. I hurried over to the corner that Kathy was standing by and looked to where she was pointing. "I see the outline of its face! Don't you see it?!?" she shrieked.

Kathy's basement had several bare light bulbs that protruded from the ceiling and were surrounded by pipes, electrical lines, and wooden framing. I approached the corner in which the demon was standing and ironically felt quite at peace. In fact, the entire time I was in Kathy's home I felt at ease. It was cozy and calm. *What was going on? Am I just worn out from this routine or was Kathy having delusions?*

"To be honest, I don't sense any demon down here, Kathy." I turned my head to tell Kathy and as I did I finally saw the truth. If I tilted my head a certain way, the shadow cast by the nearest light bulb appeared to have facelike qualities. My mind clicked and I realized what was happening to Kathy in her mind.

Quietly, I placed my finger on the cement wall and asked, "Is this the nose?"

"Yes! You see it! Everyone else didn't see it and it is so frustrating! It is right there!" Kathy exclaimed.

"And this is the mouth?" I continued.

"Yes!" Kathy was so joyous that I saw the same face she was being tormented by.

I glanced over at Mike and we all had a collective moment. Kathy was delusional or perceiving basic shadows as actual demons and apparitions of spirits. Either Kathy was having severe issues with dementia, possibly schizophrenic episodes, or some other psychological disturbance.

Everything began to make sense about the case. Her husband Josh said he had never experienced a single paranormal event in the house and although it wasn't unusual for a spouse not to experience the majority of a haunting, usually the spouse will experience at least *something* strange in the years of a haunting. The "angel wings" appeared around the same time *every day* (as the sun moves, it casts certain shadows each day). We followed Kathy back upstairs and she began to talk about the lines and symbols she saw in the grass. Mike and Carl quickly went to debunk the claims. Kathy directed them as they sought to find the exact spots where she was currently seeing the lines and symbols in the backyard.

"Over to the left more." Kathy instructed. Mike stepped forward and found in front of him a brilliant linear light—the open windows were casting it upon the grass. The lines and symbols she was seeing in her lawn were simply the reflections of the windows. How could someone mistake this as paranormal?

We continued our experiment and moved into the kitchen where Kathy had seen numbers scribbled into the floor. I kneeled down and examined the tiles. The linoleum tiles she had in her kitchen were molded to look and feel like real stone tiles. There were grooves throughout each tile piece and dirt had found its way into the creases, giving the appearance of designs and numbers. Kathy's mind perceived paranormal significance in ordinary things.

I felt sad for Kathy—to her the haunting was very much real and yet I would likely not be able to help her.

After gathering my thoughts, I took on the uncomfortable task of explaining to Kathy that what she was seeing was not paranormal. "Well, the good news is that these shadows, symbols, and numbers you are seeing are actually not paranormal. They are basic reflections and shadows, not apparitions. So that is good!" I continued. "I don't sense or feel a demonic presence here in your house. It is possible that there *was* a demonic entity or haunting here previously, however, I am not picking up on it anymore." I explained that I had felt a strange energy in the basement, but it could be caused by the high levels of electromagnetic waves from electrical lines. I suggested that Kathy have her breaker box looked at by an electrician to make sure it wasn't emitting an unhealthy EMF level.

"We can still perform a house blessing just to make sure we cover all our bases." Kathy did not appear to agree or accept our conclusion but was happy that we would still offer her and Josh a house blessing.

And so we proceeded with the house blessing, which was anticlimactic for a change. *Refreshing!* There were no paranormal reactions to our cleansing and I did not feel any resistance from a paranormal presence. It was tranquil. Kathy stated that the house blessing made her feel more at ease, which I was glad for.

I do believe in the power of house blessings as an alternative form of healing and I had hoped that it would help Kathy with her delusions and paranoia. I felt silly having Mike Best drive all the way from Indiana to help calm the nerves of a mentally unstable woman, but I knew Kathy and Josh appreciated our efforts.

After packing up our supplies I left Kathy some instructions on how to perform a basic house blessing if she ever felt that the house needed some "new and fresh energy." I also aked her to visit with her physician to discuss her experiences as they would be able to help her further. We said our goodbyes and left the house.

Just down the road was a bar and grill that the three of us decided to stop at. We needed to gather our thoughts and to share input on the case. I also wanted to catch up with Mike since I hadn't seen him in months, and it was nice to spend time together that wasn't solely focused on "casting out the ghouls."

"Well that was interesting!" Mike announced.

"Yeah, I am not sure about the validity of her paranormal sightings," Carl agreed.

"You know what makes me wonder?" I said, "If those 'phone calls' to Jason's group were actually from Kathy and she was just having a psychotic episode. And if that CJ guy in Jason's group was just faking falling down during their blessing or if there really *was* a demon and they successfully cast it out." I added, "I'm not sure."

We all concluded that at the present moment there was not a demon at Kathy and Josh's house, but it was possible that an entity had previously resided there. I remember Kathy and I talked on the phone for over an hour and a few days later she called me and asked if I had any experience with demonic cases—something we had talked about at length previously, but she had obviously forgotten completely.

I continued pointing out other possible flaws in Kathy's case. "I had to repeat several things for her. I just assumed her mind was so scattered from the stress of dealing with a demonic case, but I think she really has a mental illness. *And* nothing physical happened with this case, like her getting scratched or objects moving... I think that was a huge signal that this was all inside her mind. I had my suspicions after I first talked with Kathy, but wanted to give her story a fair chance."

As we sat in the restaurant waiting for a delicious feast we laid the paranormal topics to rest and just enjoyed ourselves as "normal people" for once. It was great. Each table had its own television and we eagerly watched the college basketball game as we stuffed our faces. Before heading our separate directions, I apologized to Carl and Mike for dragging them to a seemingly trivial case, but they just laughed it off and agreed it was great to see each other again.

On the drive home I kept mulling over the fact that Kathy's apparent illness or disorder slipped past my detection and evaluation. I always ask clients mental health questions, family history with disorders, and if they have been diagnosed with any illness. *Unless you have been diagnosed with a mental disorder, how would you know that you are just experiencing an illness's symptoms?* Kathy's answers to these questions were truthful, but they didn't accurately portray her true disorder. No, she hadn't been diagnosed, she did not have a family history of any disorders, and she was not suffering from other mental illnesses.

Sometimes our minds lead us to believe one thing, when our hearts and intuition are telling us a different story. Throughout my experience with Kathy, since the initial discussion, my gut questioned the soundness of her stories, but my mind insisted that it was likely just a very severe case and we had to help.

From dealing with Matt's stalking tendencies to Kathy's delusions of a demonic haunting, it was an interesting experience for me. Exhausted and confused, I chuckled to myself in the car and remembered that this "strangeness" came with the paranormal territory—I just always assumed it would be caused by the other side and not living humans. I was dead wrong (no pun intended).

A few weeks later, in March, Kathy wrote to me, stating that the demon and demonic shadows were still present in her home and she wanted additional help. I reassured her that the shadows were not paranormal, and to prove so, I asked her to keep a journal of what time the shadows appeared during the day. I responded in a thorough letter.

"You should see a correlation between when the shadows appear and the time of day. If you keep a journal long enough, you will see that the appearances of the shadows will also be affected by the hours of daylight as the seasons continue. I want you to go around the house with Josh and try to figure out what objects are causing each shadow. You can try to rearrange the objects so that the shadows don't resemble faces or silhouettes anymore." In regards to her request for additional help, I did not feel comfortable passing this case on to another paranormal group seeing as it was likely a mental illness problem.

> *"I am unfortunately not comfortable with forwarding your case on to someone else—the shadows you perceived to be paranormal were explainable and you have not experienced any other signs of a demonic haunting. If I were to forward your case on to someone else I would be obligated to share this information and they likely would want you to have a psychological evaluation."*

I also suggested that she follow up with performing her own house blessings every season, due to the calming effect white sage has. Perhaps it could act as a placebo as well.

A month later I received another e-mail from Kathy asking for help with the shadows—she had completely forgotten my response and explanation, never bothered to read it, or she didn't want to accept it. She had also seemingly forgotten that I left her instructions for performing her own blessing and that we had debunked all of the shadows inside her home. I wanted to help her, but the only help I really could offer was pointing her in the direction of a psychologist. I suggested that she contact me if she experienced anything physical (being scratched, doors banging, touching, and so on), but aside from that she would have to adjust to living with the shadows in her home.

Not all cases and "hauntings" are paranormal; however, the majority of my clients are truly experiencing something not of this world. In this case, Kathy had lost her ability of deductive reasoning. Most people realize that when objects or things block a light source, a shadow is generated; however, Kathy believed that these shadows were an imminent threat to her well-being. It is always a healthy practice to try to find a rational explanation for strange phenomena and to not immediately jump to paranormal conclusions. Therefore, when something truly abnormal happens, you will be able to recognize the difference.

I have not heard from Kathy since, but I hope she is finally in harmony with her home and receiving the help she needs from a medical professional.

CHAPTER 8

MY MOTHER'S ENCOUNTER

The following chapter is an experience my mother had years ago and was instrumental in stirring my curiosity about spiritual warfare and the demonic. It is the story that haunted me in my young adult life and was always a favorite "request" amongst my friends during Halloween season. My mother didn't like sharing the story because she was fearful others would not receive the story well or assume that her sanity was up for grabs. I always knew my mother was telling the truth, if only for the telltale goose bumps she had when sharing the story. I would like the story to be told in my mother's own words so she, too, can share her experience with you. I think she writes beautifully and is best at painting this dark story in your mind.

———

Long before my daughter Samantha was born, I would encounter something I would later realize was a demon. I always had psychic abilities, as do many of the women in our family; however, this was something I had never encountered, nor was prepared for.

My aunt Ilene needed help, whether she wanted to acknowledge it or not. I went to Denver, along with my mom, to do whatever was necessary to get her life back on track. We had no idea how hard that would prove to be. We did know, however, that Ilene had a problem with alcoholism. It was out of control, as was her battle with hoarding. Her life was falling apart and, as her family, we needed to help.

Ilene's daughters had taken her on vacation, allowing us to clean up the house while she was gone. Our visit and agenda was not known to Ilene but it had to be that way—Ilene would have never let us come into her home, let alone clean it for her. Her hoarding problem prevented her from throwing away a simple piece of paper; how could we have thoroughly cleaned it with her present?

Opening the back door of her quad-level home I was met with the stench of rotting food and other obscene smells. The door would only open a little because of the collection of junk and debris in its path. It was an overwhelming sight as my mom pushed against me and the door trying to get in.

"Get in!" she kept saying.

"There is *no* place *to* get!" I explained. It was true. Trash, piled as high as skyscrapers, landscaped the room. A cityscape of trash—its roads were tiny pathways. I had never seen anything like it, nor had my mom, as our eyes adjusted in the dim light of the sobering scene.

"Oh my God," she breathed behind me, her eyes wide. She stood paralyzed by the enormity of encountering her sister's real life; the one Ilene had tried so hard to conceal. It stood before us now exposed, raw, and unrelenting in its depravity and sadness. She had lived like this for decades; lived in this filth, this utter hopelessness, pretending to the outside world that all was fine. It clearly was not. Nothing was fine.

I picked my way along the paths through the teetering piles of junk, bottles, rotting food, clothes, old toys, and nameless trash. Deeper and deeper into the hoard I went, stunned by its severity. A toilet crowded to its rim in bloody tissues, its water a thick hardened crust.

The kitchen was a mass of moldy pots, dishes, cans, food, and cereal boxes staggering on top of each other. Mousetraps with mummified mice in various stages of decomposition balanced on the boxes. I heard live ones scuttle away from me in hiding. A black ooze ebbed from the refrigerator, which had stopped working months ago. Everything was rotten and had liquefied.

Every single room was blanketed in thick layers of trash. I stopped in the upper hallway to peer into the bathroom. It was unusable; the tub filled with magazines, the sink with cans and bottles from her drinking.

I started shuffling towards her bedroom when I was stopped by something I had never experienced before. Without warning, I was transported back in time. Seemingly, a movie began playing before my eyes. In front of me was my pregnant aunt, cowering on the floor of the hallway while her husband, in his drunken rage, kicked and hit her with fists as she screamed.

I watched, horrified, unable to help as he mercilessly beat her. It was only a glimpse into the horrors of her life before I was back—back in the hallway, shaking. Dazed, I tried to collect my wits. It was a psychic vision. I had seen a clip of Ilene's life and what she had actually experienced in that exact spot in the house.

From the back door of the house I heard my mother call. She had been too overwhelmed to even move past the back door. "Do you think we can do it?" The fear and uncertainty was clear in her voice.

I thought to myself, *Drop a match*—it would have been a quick solution, but I knew that wasn't the answer. We were Ilene's only chance at a normal life. If we didn't help her, no one would.

"Yeah," I tentatively answered. "We can do it."

My uncle Keith, a recovering alcoholic who was separated from Ilene and living in his own apartment, tried his best to warn us off. She was like a banshee when angry and she would be furious! He was obviously scared of her, how she would react, what she would do when she returned home. He begged us to just fly back home and leave it as it was. However, that would be a death sentence for my aunt. Someone had to help her. We had to be the help, and there was no one else.

With my mom and uncle so against tackling the job, I prayed that night for a sign from God, something to tell me this was the right thing to do, even though I dreaded it. The next morning a rainbow greeted me. Not just one rainbow, but two—a double rainbow. I knew it was my sign, the sign I often get in answer to a prayer.

We lugged bag upon bag of garbage out of the house, slinging it into the back of the car and driving off to the many dumpsters we used throughout the city. We had promised her daughters, my cousins, we would be discreet, "so the neighbors wouldn't know." We had stupidly agreed. Renting a dumpster would have been far easier, and the neighbors DID know—how could they not? Living next to them for years, they knew. The shroud of secrecy alcoholic families hide in is an illusion, their way of protecting themselves from the truth everyone else can see except them.

From early in the morning to late in the evening we worked, clearing away the debris of her broken life. In the evenings we attended alcoholic intervention sessions put on by the local hospital to understand the disease and how to encourage her to get help for herself.

My mom contacted plumbers and repairmen to get the systems in the house working again. Mom bought Ilene a new water heater and refrigerator. The old fridge, when taken away, had vomited its rotten, slimy contents on the lawn, burning the grass brown and filling the neighborhood with its stench. A fortune in bottle returns from her drink mixers was saved, along with money we found in random tin cans and other places, to give to her later. We put it in an Easter basket, the largest thing we could find. She had so very little to live on.

Days passed as we worked, exhausted and reeking, but the house was slowly getting cleaner. Next up on the list of cleaning was her bedroom. It had been a nice bedroom once. There was a matching furniture set and flowered bedspread. It was very pretty at one time, before the mice had chewed through it, and the mattress she slept on. She kept a hammer near her indent in the bed to fend them off. Thick layers of newspapers from decades past carpeted the floor. Her children's baby teeth were saved in a can on the dresser and in envelopes on the floor. Silver dollars, a wedding gift meant for me, were in a sack behind the door. In the shower was a waterfall of dead mice rotting in traps that cascaded to the drain. Horrible, it was all so horrible.

I let my mind wander, taking a break from it all, as I absentmindedly looked out the window towards the mountains. I needed to see something pretty, something peaceful. Clouds were rolling in. I watched them billow across the clear blue sky. Slowly, lazily at first, then faster and faster the clouds came, roiling into a boil. It became alarming. They churned towards the window, tumbling at me in a mad heat.

A wind blew into the room, slowly rising to a gust, then to a fierce howl. Angrily picking up pieces of paper and throwing them, the wind swirled around me, taunting. This was no ordinary gust of wind that would blow in and die down, or one that would just stream through on its way to someplace else. This wind had a purpose, a mind. What was this? It felt threatening.

It swirled faster and faster, picking up dust, debris, and papers, giving itself form until it was a confusing, terrifying whirlwind speeding all around me. Papers flapped, rattled, and snapped at my face. At first I had watched in awe, then disbelief, now in fear. My skin prickled. The hairs on my arms and neck stood straight up in sheer terror. Something I could feel but couldn't see was inside that whirling mass.

It was personal in tone and it wasn't stopping. Somehow I remembered I could, and therefore would, escape. I ran for the door. Grasping the knob I turned and pulled, expecting relief. The door didn't budge. There was *no* lock, just a regular doorknob— logically it should have opened. I turned it again, pulling harder. Harder and harder I pulled at the door. The door remained unnaturally solid, unmoving, not even flinching. I banged my fist against it, kicking it—still it didn't move. I was panicking at the thought and reality of being trapped. The whirlwind behind me grew stronger.

Terrified, I started screaming. I was screaming for all I was worth and banging furiously on the door. I felt it move. The knob turned on its own. Then the door burst open with ease into the room. My mother's worried face behind it.

"What's wron…" She stopped speaking as soon as she saw it—the angry swirling mass behind me. Her eyes and mouth flew open. Slowly, quietly, she formed the words, "What *is* that?"

"I don't know! But we're getting *out of here!*" I grabbed her hand, forcing her down the stairs with me. We didn't stop running until we reached the curb of the street.

Like dazed birds hitting a window, we stood trying to grasp what had just happened. "What *was* that?" she asked again.

"I don't know, I don't know," I kept repeating as if repetition would somehow make it clear. "We need to get away from here." That was all I knew.

The warm coffee at the coffee shop we sat in helped soothe us. Talking it over, we were as frightened and confused as before. There were no answers for what had just happened. It defied any rational explanation. All I knew was that *something* was in that house now, something angry. Whatever this thing was, it hated us, hated us for disturbing it and Ilene, its prey. It was evil, and I feared it. We didn't go back to the house for the rest of the day.

Somehow we found the courage to go back the next day and continue on with our work for the days to come. We cleaned and fixed the house up until there was no more time. Ilene was coming home that day.

When she arrived at my uncle's apartment, she eyed me suspiciously. "Why are you here?"

The people in the room scattered, anticipating the storm. I sucked up my courage and met her gaze head-on, "We've come to help you. We've cleaned your house."

I couldn't keep track of all the emotions that raced across her face, until she settled upon the one she wanted to use. It was hurt.

After all the incriminations of "How could you? Why would you do this to me? What have you done?" were played out, I explained why. She knew. She understood, but she was angry—angry and embarrassed—yet unsure how to play her hand.

In walking-on-eggshells mode, we took her over to the house. She walked through it with all of us, hesitant, unsure, yet in wonder. Amazed at the change and what had been done, she was awed. I saw genuine thankfulness in her eyes, and at times in her voice, as she commented on the work we had done. She knew it hadn't been easy and that it had been done to benefit her, not to hurt her. Still, she was overwhelmed, unsure what to do, or feel.

Ilene stayed at Keith's apartment, along with the rest of us—her daughters, mom, and me. It was a normal night—dinner, some TV, and relaxing. I hadn't had a chance to talk with her daughters about what was to happen next. I discretely gathered them into a bedroom to talk. We were going to stage an intervention for Ilene and confront her with the truth of her alcoholism. We wanted her to see we loved her, and wanted her to live the best life she could. However, in order to do that, she had to give up the alcohol. They agreed and the plan was set.

Ilene however, had been listening at the door, which none of us realized until later. In the few moments her daughters and I had been talking, she had gotten into the one bottle of whisky Keith kept in his apartment, as a reminder of his former life.

She was opening a package as I sat down next to her at the table. She grabbed the knife she had been using and held it up at me menacingly. Threatened, I stiffened, waiting on instinct. "Want to spend the night with me at *my* house?" she asked, coolly eyeing me.

Staying with her, at her house was *not* something I wanted to do, ever. I made some polite excuse as to why I didn't want to stay there *that* night, in case I was misreading her. However, she knew why, and sensed I knew too. We were talking about the darkness in her house, even though it didn't have a name. Slowly she began working herself into a rage, working toward her shrieking crescendo. Screaming, blind with rage, she demanded to go home. There was no negotiating with her. She was a ranting banshee until someone agreed to take her back home.

Over the next several days she raged in a drunken furor. We checked in on her, as she would let us; the few times she'd answer the phone. We'd been told at the alcoholic intervention training that unless she was in danger of hurting herself or someone else, there legally wasn't anything we could do. We didn't have the authority to have her committed. Keith and her daughters, who did have the authority, were too afraid of her, and refused to do what needed to be done.

Finally, calling her bluff, mom and I went over and demanded she let us in. We gave her the Easter basket full of money we'd left earlier by the back door in a failed attempt to entice her out. The money she liked. She didn't like our talk, and hurled a toaster at me, threatening both mom and myself. She was not going to stop, even if it meant her death; this was the way she wanted it, to drink herself to death. She made that very clear.

We gave her family the information we had collected from the hospital on getting her help, knowing, sadly, they would never use it, although they assured us they would. I knew while boarding the plane for home that it was the last time I would see my aunt alive. And it was—she died three years later.

Several weeks passed after I had gotten home from Ilene's house. The rest of the family and I had discussed what, if anything, could be done to help her. She needed to be committed until she could dry out and go through the program at the hospital, if anyone wanted to save her life. Sadly, those that did want to help didn't have the power to make her.

Asleep in my bed, something was bothering me, troubling me awake. I heard a voice in my head quite plainly say, "Get up, get up now! It's here!" the voice was urgent. I was fully awake in a second. That same feeling of absolute terror I had felt in Ilene's house was with me again, here, in *my* house. It *was* here! I felt "it." The hairs on my body did too. Evil and angry, it was here. It had hunted me down and found me, tracking me across the country after several weeks. Shattering the illusion of the safety of my home. It had come for me. Seeking revenge, it waited in the dark hallway, seething. My heart pounded in fear.

I heard footsteps. *It* was moving. Coming closer towards me; panic welled up in me until I felt I would burst. I couldn't fight this thing physically, I knew that. It wasn't of this world. I did the only thing I could do to protect myself; I prayed. Through my fear, I had somehow remembered what my grandmother had told me long ago. Evil spirits or demons had no power over you when you prayed and commanded them to leave in God's name. They were compelled by God's power to leave.

Over and over again I said the words in my head, "In the name of God, I command you to leave!" I said it with all the force of my being. I felt the heat of my conviction flow outward from me to the entity. Spiritual warfare, battling something I couldn't see with prayer.

In time, when I was brave enough to let down my defense, I sensed it was gone. The hair on my neck and arms was no longer standing up straight. The prickly feeling was gone. The terror was gone. *It* was gone.

In my era, one did not talk about the supernatural, the paranormal, much less demons or evil spirits. Those things were considered the ideas of a childish, immature mind. Such things didn't exist in the modern world. We were far too sophisticated to believe in old wives' tales like that. Anyone who did take such things seriously obviously had something wrong with them and needed to see a psychiatrist, perhaps on an in-patient basis.

I knew what I had experienced was real in every sense of the word, but there was no way an unbelieving world would ever acknowledge that. I kept it to myself for many years.

EPILOGUE

I hope this book enables individuals to find the assistance and guidance they are seeking. I could have written a book that idolized my efforts and only mentioned my successful cases; however, I felt it was important to mention my failures as well. You cannot save everyone, but you can help many—especially yourself.

It is not necessary to work through some ordained or holy individual—God will simply work through you if you invite Spirit into your life and heart. Great Spirit is a part of all of us—being His creations—and you have a closer connection than you might have realized. Speak to Him from your heart as if you were talking with your best friend, and ask for help when you need it. The help you request may not come in the form or timing that you expected, but you will always be provided with what you need.

Remember that there is a lesson in everything and you must constantly strive to see the big picture: our objective here on earth is to help, love, accept, and respect others. To treat this earth and its creatures with the same dignity, to go out of our way to lend a helping hand, and to spread love and positivity to others. What you put into this world is what you will receive. If we work together in such a manner, the world will change for the better. And perhaps the evil in this world will recede into the cracks and depths once more.

Some people are faced with a more difficult life path than others, and dealing with the demonic is no small feat. You must remain strong in your faith and convictions, and to work as a team with your loved ones and family members residing in the home. If you are suffering from alcoholism, substance abuse, depression, anxiety, and other troubling habits, ask God to give you the strength needed to make the changes that will improve your life. Nothing good comes from these destructive habits. The demonic love to influence you through these behaviors and participating in them gives them a foothold on your spirit and life. Stay strong.

Eat fresh and healthy foods, exercise, spend time bonding with your loved ones and family, start a garden, volunteer, or perform small acts of kindness. Remove yourself of anyone that harms you, makes you feel bad about yourself, or drains you of your energy. There are people in this world who will try to drag you down with them, but rise above their influence and surround yourself with loving and warm individuals. Keep your home and life clean. They say "cleanliness is next to Godliness." I feel this is ironically true. Clean, healthy, and functioning homes are not bogged down with negativity that attracts the demonic. Things that you do not appreciate will be taken from your life, so take pride in your home; take care of your belongings and order will follow.

Be grateful. It's hard in our industrialized world not to worry about money, get stressed over things in our daily lives and illnesses, but be grateful. Gratitude is one of the emotions that will bring you closest to God. Instead of focusing on the negative and always seeing "what is wrong," change your mindset and begin to open your eyes to all the blessings we have in our lives. Each day is a gift. Use it wisely. Will you use this gift to help others or to hurt others? Every action, every conversation, every gesture … these all effect the people around us whether we are conscious of it or not. Use that amazing ability to affect others, and put light into their lives. You will see the darkness leave your own life. Everything is cyclical; everything is connected, including ourselves. Utilize it for good and to help the world we live in.

For the paranormal investigators reading this book, not all clients are ready to let go of their bad habits (drinking, drug abuse, etc.), but you can help numerous people by performing house blessings and providing counseling. Do not investigate the unknown world for the sole purpose of gathering evidence and experiencing thrills. Your objective should be to help people and families—a much higher and nobler pursuit. Be very specific in the individuals you choose to associate and work with, make sure you are on the same page and share the same motives: to help others. Protect yourselves. The more you investigate, the more likely you will encounter the demonic. Never put yourself or others in danger.

I hope this book was enlightening. Aside from the scary stories, I hope readers saw the beauty in that the clients were able to claim back their homes and return to their lives. Anyone can do it—it just takes strength, courage, faith, love, and God's power. I wish the best for all my readers. Although this world is surrounded by darkness and trying times, look further and you will see the bounty of good. May you see the light against the dark, and may you live blessed lives.

APPENDIX A
WARFARE PRAYER

Note: As stated previously, readers are welcome to substitute "God" with their preferred name for a Higher Power.

Heavenly spirit, I bow in worship and praise before you. I cover myself with the white light and protection of God. I claim the protection of the light for my family, my finances, my home, my spirit, soul, and body. I surrender myself completely in every area of my life to you. I take a stand against all the workings of darkness and negativity that would try to hinder me and my family from best serving you. I address myself only to the true and living God who has all power and control over everything. In the name of the Lord, I command you, darkness and all evils, to leave my presence. I plead the love of our Lord.

Furthermore, in my own life today, I destroy and tear down all the strongholds of the darkness and negativity against my mind. I surrender my mind to you, blessed Holy Spirit. I affirm, heavenly Father, that you have not given me the spirit of fear but of power, and of love and of a sound mind. Therefore, I resist the spirit of fear in the name of the Lord, the Living God.

I refuse to doubt and refuse to worry because I have the authority and power over all; the power of the enemy and nothing will hurt me. I claim complete and absolute victory over the forces of darkness in the name of God, and I bind the evil and command it to let loose of my peace, joy, prosperity, and every member of my family for the glory of God and by faith I call it done.

I break and smash the strongholds that evil formed against my emotions today. I give my body to you, Lord, realizing that I am the temple of the Holy Spirit. Again, I cover myself with the white light and protection of God. I pray that the Holy Spirit would bring all the work of his mightiness into my life today. I surrender my life and possessions to you. I refuse to fear, worry, or to be discouraged in the name of God. I will not hate, envy, or show any type of bitterness towards my brothers, sisters, or my enemies. I will love them with the love God shed abroad in my heart by the Holy Spirit.

Open my eyes and show me the areas of my life that did not please you. Give me strength, grace, and wisdom to remove any sin or weight that would prevent our close fellowship. Work in me to cleanse me from all ground that would give evil a foothold against me. I claim in every way the victory of the Lord over all satanic forces in my life. I pray in the name of the Great Spirit and Heavenly Father with thanksgiving and I welcome all the ministry of the Holy Spirit.

Amen.

PRAYER TO ST. MICHAEL THE ARCHANGEL

Saint Michael the Archangel, defend us in battle, be our protection against the malice and snares of the devil. May God rebuke him, we humbly pray; and do thou, O Prince of the Heavenly host, by the power of God, thrust into hell Satan and all evil spirits who wander through the world for the ruin of souls. Amen.

PREPARING TO CAST OUT A DEMON

Samantha Harris, M.P.R.A., and the publishers are not responsible for the private cleansings of readers and those who read and use this book. Please use the following cleansing method at your own discretion or seek the help of a professional.

Removing a demonic entity from your home may seem terrifying or impossible, but it's not. You must remain positive and not fearful; demons feed off of fear and negative energy. Although we recommend recruiting the help of a minister, spiritual healer, or investigative group that performs cleansings for severe cases, it is possible to remove the entity yourself and with your family. God has given you this power.

Many individuals believe that only church-ordained individuals have the power to remove these entities, but that is false. Anyone can cast out a demon, but it requires knowledge, very firm faith in a Higher Power, and the willingness to fight the battle between good and evil (i.e., spiritual warfare). I have actually seen priests and exorcists fail at removing demonic entities and instead the client was able to cast the demon out themselves. Have faith in yourself and your Higher Power.

The following cleansing method incorporates Christian, Catholic, and Native American techniques for removing evil spirits and demonic entities. This method also helps human spirits "cross over."

First, you must figure out why the entity has come into your life. If it is from domestic violence, alcoholism, substance abuse, depression, meddling with the occult, and so on, you *must* be willing to make a lifestyle change. If you continue to drink or exhibit bad habits and behaviors, the demon will likely not leave. Remember, they prey on the weak and ill, so you must make yourself strong for the demon to leave. A healer can perform a cleansing and protect the family, but if the family is not willing to change the behavior that welcomed in the entity, it is likely that the entity will return.

Family members should have an honest meeting and discuss experiences; estimate when experiences began and try to identify what "triggered" the entity's arrival. Once you identify how and why the demon came into your life, it is easier to remove it.

Leading up to a house cleansing, you must never antagonize or challenge the demon. Simply ignore the entity and keep saying prayers out loud that command it to leave in the name of God until you are ready for a cleansing. Do not interact with the entity.

All family members must be spiritual, and believers in God/Great Spirit. If you do not believe in God or a divine being, your cleansing's results may be compromised. No specific religion or denomination is required, but you must have faith in God and ask that God come into your life and home to remove the demonic entity.

Find and schedule a time when all family members and those living within the house can gather together for an hour or two. You should always perform house cleansings during the daytime and not at night—evening cleansings are less effective in my experience. Everyone must be present during the cleansing and remain present the entire time; otherwise your cleansing may fail.

Children and animals should be present, as they will help remove the entity and can participate in the ceremony. Assign the children a particular job or allow them to help you with the steps of the ceremony. Empowering your child is critical, as they truly have the power to remove the demon and must exert their authority by helping with the ceremony.

House cleansings involve the entire home and family—you fight as a team and it builds a family bond that demons are weakened by. If one of the family members or children leaves before the ceremony, the entity can follow that individual and return home with them after the blessing is finished—and thus the haunting will continue.

Gather the following supplies for your cleansing:

- A white sage smudge stick (can be found at a new age / metaphysical bookstore or online); sustainably collected white sage is best
- A feather or feather wand (you can buy or make one)
- Charcoal discs (can be found online or at a local tobacco / hookah shop)
- Salt (you can also use sea salt)
- Olive oil
- Holy water (you can collect holy water at your local Catholic church or buy online)
- An oven-safe and fire-proof bowl to burn your white sage in; you can also buy an abalone shell to burn the white sage in if you would like to use the more traditional Native American smudging method

Print off or read the nondenominational Warfare Prayer provided at the back of this book to use at the end of the ceremony. All family members should recite the prayer together as a closing ceremony. You may also use the St. Michael prayer from appendix B, in which Michael the Archangel is invoked to help protect the family.

You *must* bless and smudge every room and corner of the house, including the basement, crawl space, attic, closets, garages, porches, decks, bathrooms, etc. For the attic area you can lift the door and waft the white sage smoke into the attic and throw salt in the attic. Be thorough.

During your cleansing, you must repeat your prayers out loud during each step and process. An example prayer is given in the ceremony instructions in appendix D.

After performing a cleansing, you must not attempt to "capture evidence" or even give thought to the haunting. Pretend that you are part of the Witness Protection Program and are beginning a new life—one without fear, without thoughts of the demonic. And never look back.

To perform the cleansing and house blessing, follow the steps listed in the following section.

THE HOUSE BLESSING/ CLEANSING CEREMONY

Open a few doors and windows throughout the house to "let the spirits out" and to prevent the white sage smoke from becoming too thick. You may close the doors and windows after the cleansing is over.

Break off pieces of the white sage smudge stick and place them in a heat-resistant bowl or abalone shell.

Light your charcoal disc on the stovetop or with a lighter, until the charcoal begins to glow orange around the bottom of the disc. *Use tongs or heat-resistant cooking utensils to safely remove the hot charcoal disc and place it on to the pieces of white sage. You can use a hot mitten to hold the bowl or shell if it becomes too hot during the ceremony. Very hot! Use caution!*

Using your feather, begin to waft the smoke around the house and in every room. Waft the smoke into closets, corners, and all areas of each room.

As you travel through the house burning the white sage, begin saying a prayer out loud in every room: *"In the name of God, I cast out any demons or evil entities in this house. You are no longer welcome here and you are no longer allowed here. In God's name I pray. Amen!"* You can also pray for positivity and blessings: *"God, I ask that you fill this house with white light, love, positivity, prosperity, good health, and happiness. May no negative energy or entities reside here anymore. Amen!"* **Repeat your prayers out loud during the entire ceremony and during each step.**

Once you have smudged all areas of the house, closets, garage, and so on, you can set the bowl and white sage in the kitchen sink. Run water over the charcoal disc and it will extinguish.

Using your olive oil bottle, dab some of the oil onto your finger and anoint above each doorway and window in the sign of the cross or a symbol of God. Keep repeating your prayers out loud and with conviction.

Grab a pinch of salt and sprinkle it in every corner of each room. Take the salt and draw a line in front of each doorway, entrance, and exit to the home. You can also sprinkle salt into each closet. Keep saying your prayers.

Take your bottle of holy water and begin walking through the house, splashing the water in the sign of the cross or a holy symbol while praying. Bless each room and sprinkle the water in all areas of the home.

After all steps have been completed, gather together as a family. All family members should command the demon(s) and spirits to leave out loud and claim their home back. Take turns telling the entity(s) to leave in the name of God.

Read the Warfare Prayer and/or St. Michael's Prayer (provided in this book) out loud as a family. All family members should obtain a copy or practice the repeat-after-me method for reading the prayer.

The spirit or entity should have departed, but you may repeat the cleansing as frequently as you like until you feel the entity has left. When an entity leaves, the house should feel lighter, brighter, and more "airy." Most people will feel a sense of peace. For severe cases, several cleansings may be required to fully remove the demon. Do not lose faith; it can be a tough and long battle but it is worth it in the end!

Give thanks to God and to each of the family members for working together to remove this entity.

Close the doors and windows after the smoke has thinned out and the cleansing is complete.

Extra Information & Techniques

You may also burn a section of a dried "sweet grass" braid after the cleansing is completed to promote positive and healing energy.

Burning Palo Santo sticks can also clear out negative energy and they are used to remove evil spirits.

I also recommend purchasing a Himalayan rock salt lamp to use as a nightlight. It is believed that demons have a harder time manifesting when there is a light present at night. The salt rock also emits ions that promote a positive environment and energy—further dispelling negative entities. They are great for creating a calm and relaxed atmosphere in your home, regardless of a negative haunting.

Some clients choose to play a gospel music or a worship CD during their cleansings to help drive out the evil spirits.

To Write to the Author

If you wish to contact the author or would like more information about this book, please write to the author in care of Llewellyn Worldwide Ltd. and we will forward your request. Both the author and publisher appreciate hearing from you and learning of your enjoyment of this book and how it has helped you. Llewellyn Worldwide Ltd. cannot guarantee that every letter written to the author can be answered, but all will be forwarded. Please write to:

Samantha E. Harris
℅ Llewellyn Worldwide
2143 Wooddale Drive
Woodbury, MN 55125-2989

Please enclose a self-addressed stamped envelope for reply, or $1.00 to cover costs. If outside the U.S.A., enclose an international postal reply coupon.

GET MORE AT LLEWELLYN.COM

Visit us online to browse hundreds of our books and decks, plus sign up to receive our e-newsletters and exclusive online offers.

- **• Free tarot readings • Spell-a-Day • Moon phases**
- **• Recipes, spells, and tips • Blogs • Encyclopedia**
- **• Author interviews, articles, and upcoming events**

GET SOCIAL WITH LLEWELLYN

Follow us on

Find us on Facebook

www.Facebook.com/LlewellynBooks

twitter™

www.Twitter.com/Llewellynbooks

GET BOOKS AT LLEWELLYN

LLEWELLYN ORDERING INFORMATION

Order online: Visit our website at www.llewellyn.com to select your books and place an order on our secure server.

Order by phone:
- Call toll free within the U.S. at 1-877-NEW-WRLD (1-877-639-9753)
- Call toll free within Canada at 1-866-NEW-WRLD (1-866-639-9753)
- We accept VISA, MasterCard, and American Express

Order by mail:
Send the full price of your order (MN residents add 6.875% sales tax) in U.S. funds, plus postage and handling to: Llewellyn Worldwide, 2143 Wooddale Drive Woodbury, MN 55125-2989

POSTAGE AND HANDLING

STANDARD (U.S. & Canada):
(Please allow 12 business days)
$25.00 and under, add $4.00.
$25.01 and over, FREE SHIPPING.

INTERNATIONAL ORDERS (airmail only):
$16.00 for one book, plus $3.00 for each additional book.

Visit us online for more shipping options.
Prices subject to change.

FREE CATALOG!

To order, call
1-877-
NEW-WRLD
ext. 8236
or visit our
website

Encounter with Hell
My Terrifying Clash with a Demonic Entity
ALEXIS MCQUILLAN

The events in this story are true, but the names and locations have been changed to protect the reader. Alexis is a psychic who never believed in demons until she came face to face with pure evil. This is her true story of battling a terrifying entity that was so powerful it turned her life upside down and put her in mortal danger...

Her nightmare begins shortly after she and her husband relocate to a small lakeside community. After hearing rumors about the nearby Matthews residence, Alexis investigates the nineteenthcentury house and its spirit inhabitants. She soon finds herself caught in a demon's snare of violent fury—subjecting her to deep growls, a malevolent force attacking her in bed, and phantom apparitions, ultimately leading to a horrific spiritual battle with a demon hell-bent on her destruction.

978-0-7387-3350-0, 216 pp., 5³⁄₁₆ x 8   **$14.99**

BATTLING DEMONS OF DARKNESS

One Man's Fight Against Evil Spirits

BRANDON BOSTON

Battling Demons of Darkness
One Man's Fight Against Evil Spirits
BRANDON BOSTON

During a seemingly ordinary Sunday church service when he was a young child, Brandon Boston experienced his first encounter with the paranormal—an exorcism. After that life-changing day, demons and dark spirits relentlessly haunted Brandon as he grew up. Now a young man determined to face his destiny, Brandon shares his true, first-hand stories of battling demons.

Join Brandon on his transformative journey from a terrified boy running from dark entities into a confident man whose purpose is to defeat them. Experience his terrifying encounters with demons. Meet the families he has helped escape their own hauntings. Discover how to fight evil spirits yourself. *Battling Demons of Darkness* will give you the inspiration needed to fight any entity of darkness in your life.

978-0-7387-3680-8, 264 pp., 5³⁄₁₆ x 8   **$14.99**

Marcus F. Griffin
Foreword by Jeff Belanger
EXTREME PARANORMAL
INVESTIGATIONS
The Blood Farm Horror,
the Legend of Primrose Road,
and Other Disturbing Hauntings

Extreme Paranormal Investigations
The Blood Farm Horror, the Legend of Primrose Road, and Other Disturbing Hauntings

Marcus F. Griffin

Set foot inside the bone-chilling, dangerous, and sometimes downright terrifying world of extreme paranormal investigations. Join Marcus F. Griffin, Wiccan priest and founder of Witches in Search of the Paranormal (WISP), as he and his team explore the Midwest's most haunted properties. These investigations include the creepiest-of-thecreepy cases WISP has tackled over the years, many of them in locations that had never before been investigated. These true-case files include investigations of Okie Pinokie and the Demon Pillar Pigs, the Ghost Children of Munchkinland Cemetery, and the Legend of Primrose Road. Readers will also get an inside glimpse of previously inaccessible places, such as the former Jeffrey Dahmer property as WISP searches for the notorious serial killer's spirit, and the farm that belonged to Belle Gunness, America's first female serial killer and the perpetrator of the Blood Farm Horror.

978-0-7387-2697-7, 264 pp., 5³⁄₁₆ x 8　　　　**$15.95**

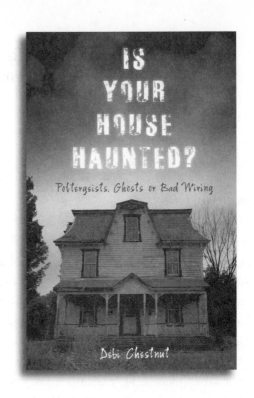

IS YOUR HOUSE HAUNTED?

Poltergeists, Ghosts or Bad Wiring

Debi Chestnut

Is Your House Haunted?
Poltergeists, Ghosts or Bad Wiring
Debi Chestnut

A door slams shut by itself, pets are acting strangely, inexplicable smells and sounds are invading your home … and you're terrified. Is there a logical explanation, or do you have a real-life ghost on your hands?

There's no reason to live in fear. This no-nonsense beginner's guide offers reassurance and practical advice on identifying—and putting a stop to—any paranormal activity that's creeping you out. Discover how to rule out any earthly explanations for strange phenomena. A comprehensive overview of all kinds of hauntings and ghosts—from aggressive poltergeists to harmless family spirits to malevolent demons—will help you understand and identify your unearthly houseguest. If you still want to banish your ghost, you'll find plenty of simple, effective techniques to get the job done.

Is Your House Haunted? also offers advice on how to talk to children about ghosts and when it might be necessary to call in paranormal experts.

978-0-7387-2681-6, 240 pp., 5³⁄₁₆ x 8   **$14.95**

STEVEN LaCHANCE

with LAURA LONG-HELBIG

THE

UNINVITED

The True Story

of the

Union Screaming House

The Uninvited
The True Story of the Union Screaming House
STEVEN A. LACHANCE

Its screams still wake me from sleep. I see the faceless man standing in that basement washing away the blood from his naked body.

Steven LaChance was forever transformed by the paranormal attacks that drove him and his family from their home in Union, Missouri. When another family falls victim to the same dark entity, Steven returns to the dreaded house to offer aid and find healing.

Paranormal investigators, psychics, and priests are consulted, but no relief is found. The demon's presence—screams, growls, putrid odors, invisible shoves, bites, and other physical violations—only grow worse. LaChance chronicles how this supernatural predator infects those around it. But the one who suffers most is the current homeowner, Helen. When the entity takes possession and urges Helen toward murder and madness, LaChance must engage in a hair-raising battle for her soul.

The Uninvited is a true and terrifying tale of extreme haunting, demon possession, and an epic struggle between good and evil.

978-0-7387-1357-1, 264 pp., 6 x 9   **$16.95**